HOW TO "I DO"

PLANNING THE ULTIMATE WEDDING IN SIX WEEKENDS OR LESS

HOLLY LEFEVRE and CHRISTINE CUDANES

ReganBooks
An Imprint of HarperCollins*Publishers*

HarperCollins books may be purchased for educational, business, or sales promotional use. For information please write: Special Markets Department, HarperCollins Publishers, Inc., 10 East 53rd Street, New York, NY 10022.

FIRST EDITION

Designed by Robin Arzt

Library of Congress cataloging-in-publication data available upon request.

ISBN 0-06-098816-9

99 00 01 02 03 ❖ 10 9 8 7 6 5 4 3 2 1

For Brett, the love of my life,
and my parents for always providing
unconditional love and support.

—*Holly Christine Lefevre*

To my parents, Jim and Cathy,
for generously giving me the
opportunity to plan my own wedding,
and my husband, Scott,
for lovingly giving me the reason to plan it.

—*Christine Cudanes*

Contents

Chapter Four CREATIVE PLANNING 34

Chapter Five THE SIX-WEEKEND WEDDING PLANNER 55

Contents ix

Chapter Eight THE BIG DAY 214

Chapter Nine THE HONEYMOON 225

Chapter Ten WRAPPING THINGS UP 235

Appendix: Wedding Info at a Glance 245

Acknowledgments

The authors would like to thank the many associates, friends, and family whose talents, comments, suggestions, and support meant so much to us as we were creating this book. Without the guidance of B. K. Nelson, and the foresight of Judith Regan, this book would never have gotten off the ground. A special thanks goes out to our editors, Amye Dyer and Cassie Jones, for their enthusiasm and constant support of the project, and to everyone at ReganBooks whose attention to detail, technical skills, and creative vision made this book what it is today.

We would also like to thank all of the people who have ever invited us to their wedding, asked us to be members of their wedding party, or shared their personal wedding experiences with us.

Our heartfelt appreciation goes out to all of our "research assistants" for supporting us during our own wedding planning experiences and throughout the writing of this book: Joyce and Richard Arenas; June Brill; Brad Christmas; Jason Crawshaw; Jan Cudanes; Cathy and Jim Cudanes; Argel Dionio; Holly Doan, Holly Doan Floral Design; Kiwi Dog; Tara Flynn; Gary Gaulton; Sandra and Robert Goldman; Todd Goldman; Tiffany Harris and

Cindy Wagner-Kenney (the best troubleshooters in town); Tina T. Hook, president of Park Avenue Bride and founder of The Independent Wedding Consultants of America; Jeanna Hosford; Veronica Knoche; Robert Korotky; Beverly LaRock; Paul LaRock; Shirley LaRock; Albert Lau; Denise LaVerde; Lynn and Dennis Lefevre; Ashley, Anthony, and Amanda Marquez; Michael Moon; Bob Newell; Surekha and Rob Pessis; Diane Riddell, Creative Locations; Lauren and John Alexander Roberson; Marco Schnabel; Heather Spaizman; Ako "Kelly" Tsutagawa; Keith Vallot, Keith Vallot Photography; Lesley and Jan Vlietstra; and John Wang.

Of course none of this would have been possible without our "research subjects," our loving and supportive husbands, Brett and Scott.

Introduction

Are you ready to make the trip down the aisle? Of course—you found the right guy, he popped the question, and you're wearing the coveted ring. Everywhere you go people are offering their congratulations, but before you can even conjure up visions of bridesmaids dancing in your head, reality sets in—caterers and DJs, bouquets and boutonnieres, guest lists and invitations. If the prospect of planning your wedding leaves you wondering "Who has time for all of this anyway?" look no further than *How to "I Do."*

As recent brides, we know all too well the demands that planning a wedding can place on a newly engaged couple. When it came time to plan our own weddings, we were already juggling a myriad of professional and personal commitments, and suddenly we were faced with finding the time to plan the weddings we had always dreamed of. Through our own personal experiences as bridesmaids and finally as brides, we learned many effective methods for making every free moment count.

Consequently, we have formulated a guide that will take you through the different stages of planning a wedding, utilizing all of the information we wished we had access to when we were planning our own. *How to "I Do"* takes the guesswork out of weddings and provides you with a system of planning that fits into your life—without taking it over. In just weeks, you will complete your wedding planning without missing one important detail.

HOW TO USE THIS BOOK

Throughout *How to "I Do,"* we take the busy bride by the hand and guide her through all of the essential elements of wedding planning. This book is truly a "how-to" guide. Unlike other planners, *How to "I Do"* is written in the order you will need to read it. No more flipping through pages wondering "What do I do first?" The three distinct sections of the book not only tell you what needs to be done, but how to do it.

The first section of the book prepares you for the six weekends of planning that lie ahead of you. We will acquaint you with various organizational methods, direct you to finding the right information, and offer helpful hints on how to manage it all. This section will also guide you in making the stylistic and budgetary decisions that will impact the rest of your wedding planning.

Following is the Six-Weekend Wedding Planner. Here, everything you need to create your dream wedding is broken down into manageable sets of weekend goals—perfect for fitting into a working woman's schedule. Each section begins with a checklist of goals to accomplish during a particular weekend, and is followed by a plan of attack for accomplishing them. Everything from hiring a caterer to purchasing the gown of your dreams is covered. (Please see page 55 for further explanation of how to fully utilize the Six-Weekend Wedding Planner.)

The third section of the book guides you through the final details and shows you how to "pull it all together." Among other things, you will create a wedding day itinerary and learn how to run your own rehearsal. A complete guide to confirming and finalizing the details is also included. We prepare you, your groom, and your wedding party for the "big day" with checklists and advice. And finally, we guide you on to your sweet reward— the honeymoon.

With prime locations and vendors getting booked up so far in advance, it is advisable to begin your planning as soon as possible, whether your wedding date is twelve months or twelve weeks away. By committing yourself to six solid weekends of planning (in addition to a few weeks before and after), you can safely accomplish everything you need to do for your wedding, and still have time for life's other activities.

Even though *How to "I Do"* may look pretty, it is designed for you to use and abuse. Consider it your wedding textbook. Take notes in it, write in the margins, and highlight important information. Special worksheet sections are at the end of almost every chapter and weekend section. These worksheets are provided for you to use to keep track of important information. These can later be photocopied and taken with you as needed. Do whatever works best for you.

There is so much information contained within these covers that it could seem overwhelming at times, but absorb what you need to, and then move on. This book's quick-reading format will allow you to easily skim through the information and ideas—reading as little or as much as you need to accomplish the particular task at hand.

Though the book was written by brides, for brides, there are numerous sections that are meant to be shared with the groom, or members of your family, as well as the wedding party. While you may be doing most of the planning yourself, you can always benefit from the help of the members of your wedding team.

So have fun, relax, and enjoy creating your perfect wedding day. Always keep in mind the true purpose of all this planning—to marry the one you love!

1
Organize, Organize, Organize

With an engagement comes a buzz of excitement, a whirlwind of activity, a zeal to jump right into the planning—but you must not overlook the importance of getting organized! In the weeks and months leading up to your wedding date, it will be easy to get lost among the fabric swatches and menu selections. It is not uncommon for brides to wonder how they will manage it all. The answer is to establish an organizational system early on. Such a system will become your new "best friend," as it will save you time, headaches, and frustration.

There are many ways to keep accurate records and track your planning progress. Outlined in the following chapter are effective organizational methods that are easy to establish and maintain. It is helpful to use a combination of these methods, as each has a different purpose. For example, you should keep permanent records of original contracts and paperwork in the At-Home File System, travel with the Wedding Binder, and log appointments and payments on the Calendar.

THE WEDDING FILES

The At-Home File System

Establishing an At-Home File System is one of the first and most important steps in your wedding planning, as this system is used to house the original paperwork and contracts you sign throughout the planning process. It is important to keep these files at home in a safe place, not only for the sake of organization but because you do not want to lose or misplace the original contracts or agreements.

This basic organizational system is more than worth the small amount of time it takes to get it established. Setting up the At-Home File System requires the same equipment you would need for any office filing system: file folders, labels for the folders, and some type of filing unit.

Use the following steps to set up your At-Home File System:

1. Label the folders by generic categories—locations, photographers, florists, etc.
2. As you meet with vendors, file their information in the proper category, keeping each vendor's paperwork stapled or paper clipped together.
3. Once you begin making your final decisions and signing contracts, create individual folders for each of these vendors, and file the folders alphabetically.
4. Remove the other vendors' information from that section, and create a "rejection" file. Keep the rejections in a separate section of your At-Home File System. Do not throw this information out quite yet, as it may prove helpful down the line.

You may want to include other particulars in your file, but this is a list of the "must haves":

- Original paperwork or brochures from vendors or from wedding-related products.
- Your original copy of the signed contract, as well as any supplemental agreements made after the original contract was signed.
- Any other paperwork the vendor provides you, or you provide them, such as special rules for the reception location.

- Any special information you would like to share with them, or have passed along to them previously, such as magazine photos of a particular cake, bouquet, etc.

If you will be making most of your wedding planning calls from home, keep a phone log directly on the corresponding folder, or attach a separate sheet inside the folder for this purpose. Include the date, time, and purpose of the call. On the front of the folder, you may also want to list your deposit amount, amount still due, and the due date of subsequent and/or final payments. With this information in place, you can easily keep abreast of the status of your account.

The Calendar

In addition to the At-Home File System, you may want to purchase a large desk calendar. These calendars have plenty of room to write notes and messages under particular dates, and can be used to keep track of appointments, wedding-related activities, and payment due dates. Keep this calendar at home and in easy view so that you are aware of upcoming events, and so your fiancé and/or parents can also refer to it.

As you sign contracts and begin making deposits, make note of them on the calendar. Clearly mark when subsequent or final payments are due and when any remaining paperwork must be completed. If you are mailing these payments out, you may also want to note by which date these need to be sent.

PORTABLE PLANNING

While many vendors will come to your home or place of work for consultations, there are certain aspects of planning that just cannot be accomplished from either of these locations. For example, when choosing a reception location, a personal visit to the site is necessary to determine if it is right for you. In these instances, it is necessary to take your planning on the road. This part of the organizational system is set up to keep you organized and prepared no matter where you may be.

The Wedding Notebook

The first type of Portable Planning system is a notebook. This does not have to be fancy—just a spiral-bound notebook you can buy at a grocery or convenience store. You will want this notebook to have enough pages to take you through your wedding planning. A 6" x 9½" spiral notebook with at least 150 pages works well. A notebook this size can be slipped in your purse or briefcase and taken anywhere.

Use the following steps to set up your notebook:

1. Mark "WEDDING" clearly on the front cover, or buy one with a brightly colored cover, so you can spot it easily, and it will not get lost in any other paperwork you may have around the house or office.
2. Buy a notebook with dividers, or attach self-stick removable notes (Post-It Notes) to the pages as makeshift tab dividers. Leave about a ½" overhang and write the section name on this part of the note. Label these sections:

   - Calendar

   - Budget

   - Ceremony/Reception Locations

   - Attire

   - Baker

   - Beauty (Hair and Makeup)

   - Bridal Registry

   - Caterer

   - Disc Jockeys/Bands/Entertainment

   - Florists

   - Honeymoon

   - Ideas/Inspirations

   - Jewelers

   - Officiant

- Photographers

- Rentals

- Transportation

- Videographers

- Wedding Consultants

- Miscellaneous Information (Phone Log, Comments)

Each entry in the notebook should begin with the vendor's name, phone number, fax number, and contact person. Leave a blank page or two for each vendor. Use these pages to take notes as you make the initial phone contact. When and if you decide to meet with that vendor, continue with your note taking, and record any additional information the vendor may give you during this meeting.

The Wedding Binder

Instead of using a notebook, an alternative method of Portable Planning would be a Wedding Binder. It, too, requires very few pieces of equipment. You will need a 2½" three-ring binder, and top loading sheet protectors (available at office supply stores). For a more economical version of this system, you may also assemble the binder using card stock and pasting or taping pictures or photographs onto the pages.

Use these steps to set up your Wedding Binder:

1. Photocopy the weekly and master checklists from the book. Put them in the front of the binder.
2. Section the binder into pertinent categories using tab dividers. Generic categories—flowers, wedding dresses, menu ideas, etc.—work well in the beginning.
3. Load the photographs or the pictures you will be collecting from bridal magazines or friends (see Chapter Two) into the sheet protectors, and file them in the appropriate section. As you meet with vendors, you will have a visual example to present to them. The sheet protectors work well because the pictures are protected, and you can also store brochures and actual samples, such as wedding programs, in them.

4. Place the vendor's information (business cards, brochures, etc.) into the sheet protectors and file it in the appropriate category. Once you begin making decisions, you can create a specific section for that vendor and remove the information from vendors that you will not be using.
5. Photocopy the "Questions to Ask" worksheets and the checklists found throughout the book. Once you have filled out the worksheets or completed a particular goal, file the sheets in the appropriate section of the binder.
6. After you sign a contract, make a copy and load it into a sheet protector. Always keep the original in your At-Home File System.

On your wedding day, it is a good idea to have copies of all contracts, paperwork, and ideas you have discussed with each vendor, as well as other important visual and logistical matters pertaining to the wedding festivities. You will want a complete record like this in case there is a problem or miscommunication or to simply ensure you are getting what you paid for. If you continually update your Wedding Binder, by the time you reach your wedding day, you will have compiled a complete reference book containing all your final plans.

The Portable Wedding Files

A third option to consider for your Portable Planning is virtually a portable version of your At-Home File System. This requires an expandable file organizer, individual file folders, and labels. Organize this portable file in the same manner used for your At-Home File System, except do not include original contracts. Make copies and carry those with you.

WEDDING PLANNING WITH A COMPUTER

Computers are an integral part of our lives, both personally and professionally. Many busy professionals use their personal computers to keep their business and social calendars in check. For the computer literate bride and groom, computers are an ideal wedding planning tool.

E-mail

One of the easiest and most convenient ways to communicate with the wedding party, family, and even vendors, is by E-mail. With E-mail, it takes only a couple of minutes to compose a message and send it off to all of the interested parties.

Compile a list of E-mail addresses for the members of the wedding party using the Wedding Party Roster (see page 49). You will also want to get the E-mail addresses of other involved friends and family members, as well as the E-mail addresses for your vendors.

Once you have this information at hand, you can use E-mail to keep everyone periodically updated on the progress of the planning, and to pass along important messages and information. E-mail is an especially great way to exchange vital information with out-of-towners. Exchanging information with your wedding vendors via E-mail is not only a convenient means of communication, but it also leaves both parties with a written record of the "conversation."

Wedding Planning Software

A quick stop on the information superhighway is the best way to acquaint yourself with the array of wedding planning software available. You may want to try your local electronics or computer store as well. A typical program averages $35. Each program includes basic planning features, as well as additional ones unique to that program. You will have to do some further investigating to determine which program accommodates your needs.

Using the Internet, you will be able to sample much of the wedding planning software that is available. With the help of a search engine, look up "wedding planning software." By accessing a software company's web site, you can view the features each wedding planning program offers, as well as see a sample of how the system is organized. Typically, software companies have a free trial version of their program available on-line that you can download and examine. Should you discover a program that you particularly like, you can order it on-line or through the company's toll-free number.

Most wedding planning software includes the following categories:

- Bridal Attire
- Budget
- Calendar/Scheduler
- Ceremony
- Guest List/Guest Addresses
- Reception
- To-Do or Task List
- Vendors/Services

Specialized features that some programs include are the ability to:

- Track payment due dates and automatically alert you as they approach.
- Update the budget information automatically each time you make additions or subtractions.
- Organize the guest list and track the guest count.
- Automatically schedule the planning for you, according to your wedding date.
- Print the inner and outer envelopes of the invitations straight from the guest list information you have already logged in.

Other Ways to Use Your Computer

Perhaps purchasing specialized wedding planning software, or even using your computer to this extent is not what you had in mind. There are many ways to use the software already on your computer while you are planning your wedding. For example, use a spreadsheet program to track payments and keep an eye on the budget.

Additionally, you may also want to create a wedding "folder" on your computer. Use the folder to file letters, faxes, memos, and any additional communications you may compose on the computer. Confirmation letters (see page 205) can also be managed this way, by creating a generic format to be used for all of the vendors, and adding specific information as necessary.

Finally, planning and organization are not the only means to utilize your computer. You can create place cards, wedding programs, menu cards, and address envelopes with the help of a computer. There are many programs you can purchase with clip art and fonts to complement the software with which you are already working. There are kits and programs available to make your own invitations as well. Browse through the software section at your local computer or office supply store to learn more about these products.

2

Finding the Right Information

The average cost of a formal wedding rivals that of purchasing a new car. As you can see, a wedding is a large investment of time *and* money for you, your fiancé, and your families. Therefore, it deserves the same attention given to other major investments and purchases in your lives.

At first the task may seem daunting—bridal magazines as thick as college textbooks, thousands of wedding-related web sites, and advice coming at you from all angles. Taking some time to gather your thoughts and acquaint yourself with the world of wedding cakes and caterers will be of great benefit to you.

Using the tools and techniques outlined in this chapter, you will be on your way to finding the quality wedding professionals, products, and services that you need to make your wedding day a success.

THE REAL SCOOP
ON BRIDAL MAGAZINES

Bridal magazines have proven to be a tried-and-true resource for brides-to-be. They not only provide brides with facts and figures, they also inspire brides with fabulous photographs and magnificent ideas. With a little bit of reading and a few dollars, it is easy to acquaint yourself with the realm of weddings. (Please consult the Appendix for a list of bridal publications.)

The Facts

There are two main categories for bridal magazines: national and regional editions. National bridal magazines provide a "round-up" of what's going on around the country. They are quite thick, often containing between 400 and 1,000 pages, and offer a wide range of ideas and products, as well as editorial features.

Ads for bridal gowns and other bridal attire make up a large portion of the national magazines. Coverage also includes features on basic planning, etiquette, budgeting, honeymoons, home life, and marital relations. Additionally, there are special-interest national magazines. These magazines appeal to customers of particular cultural and ethnic groups, religious affiliations, and lifestyles.

On the other hand, regional magazines provide localized and specific coverage of resources in your geographical area. They are best at providing extensive coverage of and ads for local wedding professionals and services. Regional magazines provide brides in their respective areas with vast amounts of helpful information, including reception and ceremony locations, and regional trends. They cover many of the same planning and home life topics found in national magazines; however, their coverage is more in tune to the happenings within your region.

Also, regularly published lifestyle and home magazines produce special issues or editions with a focus on weddings. Special editions are wonderful for the ideas and inspiration they provide today's stylish bride and groom. Generally, special editions concentrate on ideas and inspirations from society, celebrity, and royal weddings.

Each magazine is unique in its own way. While establishing your wedding library, it is recommended to purchase at least one national magazine, for a broad perspective on weddings, and one regional magazine, to focus on your specific area. As you pursue your planning, special issues are a great source of inspiration, and provide many new and unique ideas for your wedding.

Creative Ways to Use Bridal Magazines

Bridal magazines have many advantages that are often overlooked. Literally, in your hands, you hold the key to designing your ideal wedding. Follow the simple tips below to take full advantage of all that bridal magazines have to offer:

- After setting up your organizational system (Chapter One), start a collection of magazine photos. Wedding attire, bouquet ideas, wedding cakes, decorations, and numerous other details that strike your fancy can be found in bridal magazines. These photos can be passed on to vendors and any other persons who will be responsible for creating a visual image for you on your wedding day. Always keep a copy for yourself.
- Gown shopping can be overwhelming. Go prepared! Before you begin shopping for your wedding dress, or other wedding attire, gather pictures from the magazines of the styles that appeal to you. Show these to the bridal consultant at the bridal salon or dress shop to give her an idea of your personal taste and style. None of these gowns may end up being the dress you purchase, but it gives you and the bridal consultant a good starting point.
- There are many wonderful photographs throughout the pages of bridal magazines. Tear out or mark the pages with the photographic styles and poses that appeal to you. Show these to photographers to give them an idea of the look you are striving for in your wedding day photos. Save these and go over them with the photographer once the wedding day draws closer.
- Keep out-of-town family and wedding party members in the loop. Once you have made some stylistic decisions about your wedding, you can mail color copies of representative photographs to interested family or wedding party members who live out of the area. Or, if your selec-

tion is featured in a national bridal magazine, you can tell these special people, "Look on page 64 of *Modern Bride*. That is the dress I have chosen for the bridesmaids."

- Use the reader response cards or call the toll-free numbers listed in the advertisements to request catalogs for invitations, wedding accessories, and other wedding products. This will help prepare you for some of the work you have to do during The Six Weekends.

REFERRALS, REFERRALS, REFERRALS

Referrals can be one of the best and most effective ways to find quality wedding professionals. Once you announce your engagement, friends, relatives, even strangers will share information and wedding stories with you. If you know what to look and listen for, you can greatly benefit from the "advice" that is being cast your way.

You can truly benefit from listening to the people you trust. Recently married friends or family members are some of the best sources of information you have at your disposal. Inquire about the vendors they used, what they liked or didn't like, the quality of service, and if they would consider hiring them for future events. Don't forget to ask your friends for the names and numbers of these professionals.

At a first meeting with a vendor, you will receive enormous amounts of information. One of the tools the service should provide you with is a reference or referral list. The list contains the names and phone numbers of other, noncompeting wedding professionals who can vouch for the quality of the vendor's product or service. The list may also include the names and phone numbers of recent brides for whom they have worked.

Use the list like you would any other reference list. Call a few of the professionals listed and ask questions about the prospective vendor's work or his service. Keep in mind a vendor is not going to put someone on this list who will give him a poor rating. You can also use the list as a starting point for gathering information on other services. If one vendor is trustworthy and respected, chances are he works with the same caliber of people.

If you are using a wedding consultant, she will be able to refer you to wedding professionals from a pool of vendors she works with on a regular basis. The consultant has an ongoing relationship with these vendors and can provide you with specific information, such as prices and the range of services offered, before you even meet with the vendor. When a consultant refers a vendor to you, she is putting her name on the line. A poor performance from a vendor reflects poorly on the consultant. Because of this, her list usually consists of trustworthy, reliable professionals who perform their jobs well.

Many reception sites will provide you with a list of vendors. These lists consist of vendors who work with that location on a regular basis. While you are not necessarily obligated to make selections from this list, the site may require approval for any vendors not on their list that you choose to bring in. You may run across some sites that have more severe restrictions. They require you to select all of your vendors from their approved list. Whether or not you choose to have your reception at that location, you can still utilize the list in your search for additional wedding professionals.

When using referrals, there are a few things you should keep in mind:

- If you have been referred to a prospective vendor, be sure to mention this during the initial phone call and repeat this at the first meeting. Vendors may give you a discount for being a referral.
- Referral fees or commissions (kickbacks) do exist between vendors. Don't be pressured into using vendors that are recommended by other vendors or consultants. Your comfort level, not theirs, is what's most important.

THE INTERNET

As a busy bride, you have a fabulous wedding planning resource at your disposal—the Internet. There are thousands and thousands of wedding-related web sites on the World Wide Web. If you know what to look for and where to begin, this can be an invaluable and timesaving resource right in your own home, available whenever you want or need it.

The Internet can be used for locating numerous products and services for your wedding. Wedding web sites offer planning and etiquette advice, checklists and charts, photos of wedding gowns, tips, and relationship advice. Be aware that there is an enormous amount of information available on the Internet. However, with a little patience and a plan of attack, the Internet can be an effective planning and research tool.

If you do not know exactly where to begin your search, or you would simply like to explore your options, use a search engine. Looking up the general term "weddings" will provide you with a potpourri of information—everything from wedding gowns to photographers to the meaning of flowers. For a narrower search, be as specific as possible. For example, if you are looking for a wedding consultant in the Los Angeles area, type in "wedding consultants in Los Angeles."

For a unique perspective on planning, visit the web sites of newly engaged or newly married couples. The sites contain personal stories, helpful tips, and photos, as well as planning and budgeting advice that these couples found useful. Way Cool Weddings (www.waycoolweddings.com) is a web site that showcases individual couples' personal wedding web sites. To find other personal wedding web sites, you will again need to look up "weddings" using a search engine, and then start exploring.

The *How to "I Do"* web site (www.howtoidoweddings.com) is also a great way to get started. Check it out for up-to-the-minute advice, trends, and planning information, as well as links to some of our favorite wedding web sites. (Web addresses for these sites may also be found in the Appendix on page 246.) When you find a site you like, don't forget to "bookmark" it for easy access later.

What's Available On-line

The following are examples of additional information available to you on the Internet:

- Biblical Verses, Poetry, and Songs
- Bridal Magazines
- Bridal Shows
- Chat Rooms or News Groups
- On-line Gift Registries
- Travel
- Wedding Product Catalogs
- Wedding Vendors

BRIDAL SHOWS

Bridal shows are a great source of information and ideas. These events showcase wedding professionals, as well as wedding-related products and services. They come in all different sizes, and are tailored to fit the needs of brides and grooms.

Bridal shows are time- and cost-effective, as they gather a large selection of vendors under one roof. Attending a bridal show will provide you with a little taste of everything involved in planning a wedding. This is also a great chance to see samples of several vendors' work, taste their food or pastries, and briefly meet with and ask questions of them. Many vendors offer show specials or incentives if you book with them at the show, or soon after.

If you go prepared, bridal shows can provide you with a wealth of resources and ideas for your big day. There will be numerous products and companies for you to consider. A sampling of what to expect includes: bridal gowns, bakers, caterers, photographers, makeup artists, florists, disc jockeys, bands, reception sites, rental companies, tuxedo rentals, bridesmaid dresses, gift registries, honeymoon ideas, floral preservation, transportation, financial planners, and almost anything else you could possibly use for your new life.

Bridal shows are held at hotels or convention centers, although some smaller events are held in shopping centers. Admission for most major bridal shows runs from $5 to $10, depending on the show and geographic region. Some shows offer discounts if you purchase tickets or make reservations in advance. Department stores also host wedding-related events, usually designed to entice you to register with the store for your wedding gifts. Department store or mall events are often free of charge. Look for specific admission information in the show advertisements in bridal magazines.

Bridal shows are held year-round. Listings for national events can be found in most national bridal magazines. Regional bridal magazines also list national shows and events, but additionally include advertisements for specialized shows in your geographic region. Local newspapers, wedding planning and resource centers, local radio stations, and the Internet are other sources for this information.

When attending a bridal show, you will be asked to fill out a registration card and contest entry blanks. These registration lists are made available to the vendors participating in the bridal show. You will receive mailings, and possibly phone calls, from vendors offering discounts or other promotions after the show.

Go Prepared

Attending the show as an informed and prepared bride-to-be is important. You will be walking a lot, so wear comfortable shoes, which will help keep your mind on the task at hand, not your aching feet. Using a backpack is also wise. You will be collecting brochures, business cards, and flyers all day, and a backpack will free up your hands.

Some other essentials to take with you to a bridal show include:

- **A Notebook:** To jot down ideas, information, and comments and/or a clipboard for a stable, portable writing surface.
- **A Camera:** We have never experienced a problem with this. If for some reason the show planners do not allow photos, respect their rules. ALWAYS ask a vendor before you take a photo. Some may not allow or like their product photographed. You may even want to call the show organizers for specific rules regarding photography.
- **Preprinted Address Labels:** You can use the mail order type or print some on your computer. If you are printing your own, include your wedding date, as most vendors will ask for this information as well. Vendors will ask you to fill out information cards, contest entry cards, or sign their "guest books." Having these labels will save you time. Some of the larger bridal shows provide labels for brides as they check in (for a small additional fee).

Surviving the Bridal Show Experience

Bridal shows can be overwhelming. There is a lot of activity and commotion. Music is playing, vendors are asking you questions as you walk by, handing you flyers, and pushing their product. You can survive this maze and get the most out of your bridal show experience by following a few easy steps:

- **Simplify.** Take only one person with you. Unless your groom is really tolerant and into the whole wedding planning process, it is best to have just one person go with you. Ask your mother, sister, or Maid/Matron of Honor to accompany you.

- **Have a plan.** There is usually quite a buzz of activity toward the front part of the show. If you work your way from back to front, there will be fewer people, and by the time you get back around to the more hectic part of the show, you will be accustomed to all of the activity and excitement.
- **Take your time.** Use this fabulous resource to your advantage. Allow yourself a few hours to go through the show. Go slow and take it all in. Look at samples and displays, pick up brochures, and get prices.
- **Take a break.** Most events have fashion shows every hour or so. It gives you a good break from walking around, as well as a chance to collect your thoughts. You may also get some great ideas for outfitting yourself, the groom, and the wedding party. If there are no fashion shows on the agenda, take a moment for lunch or a snack.
- **Take a second look.** Walking the show one more time will give you the opportunity to ask additional questions that may have come to mind, and to reconsider any items you may have missed on the first go-round.

Getting the Most Out of the Event

The whole purpose of attending a bridal show is to collect information and to actually see a vendor's product. Here are a few ways to do just that:

- Take notes on the brochure or flyer the vendor supplies. This way it's easy to keep the right information with the right name.
- Pay attention to the vendors' product, how they show it, and what their booth looks like. This all says a lot about their style and how they do business.
- Be sure to get the show's program or guide. It lists the participating vendors, and often has great advice and tips inside.
- Most shows offer free copies of bridal magazines to paying attendees. Definitely do not leave without picking one up.

WEDDING PLANNING AND RESOURCE CENTERS

Wedding planning and resource centers are a growing trend in the wedding industry. Centers such as A Legendary Affair in Manhattan Beach, California, are a blessing for today's busy bride. At a wedding planning center such as this, you can virtually plan your entire celebration from one location.

Think of these centers as your "wedding library." They provide a unique type of referral service, as they offer the opportunity to preview the work of many wedding professionals at one time and in one location. You can view a vendor's portfolio of work, which may include videotape samples, photos, or the actual product. Many also have lists of reception and ceremony locations. One great advantage of these centers is the opportunity to view and compare the work and prices of many vendors without any sales pressure. From here, you can make a decision as to which vendors fit into your budget and reflect your wedding style.

Another type of wedding planning center is the equivalent of a wedding-only retail store. These centers carry wedding-related products available for immediate purchase or order. Available services and products may include, but are not limited to, invitations, bridal gowns, bridal accessories, attendants' gifts, and wedding day accessories.

Most wedding centers are free of charge because their income is derived from the sale of their products or from fees paid by the vendors who are represented. Consult advertisements in regional bridal magazines for leads to wedding planning and resource centers in your area.

Before you go, call to see if an appointment is necessary and to confirm the specifics of how the wedding center functions. As well, have the basics of your wedding planning arranged. Know the approximate date, budget, and style of the wedding (see Chapter Three). And finally, always be prepared to meet in person at a later date with any vendors that interest you.

3

First Things First

The first of many questions you will be asked once you announce your engagement is "When's the big day?" Next comes a plethora of other stylistic inquiries. "What kind of wedding will it be? Will it be an evening or afternoon wedding? Formal or casual?" And this is just from friends, family, and strangers. Whirling around in your mind are a whole other set of questions. How much do flowers cost? What type of photography do we want? Do I need a wedding consultant? What kind of wedding do we want? And maybe most important, who is going to pay for all of this?

The questions are endless, and so are the options. So, before you jump into planning your wedding, there are some crucial matters to discuss. These are the types of subjects that will affect your planning and decision making from this day forward. Outlined in the following chapter are important questions that need to be asked and answered before you interview your first vendor or put down your first deposit.

SET THE DATE

Choosing a date will set the framework for your wedding. For a December wedding, you may choose to reflect the festive atmosphere that comes along with the holidays. Or, maybe you *have to have* tulips in your bouquet. If so, unless you have a large budget, it is practical to plan a spring wedding, when tulips are in season. These are just two examples showing the importance of selecting an appropriate wedding date.

The following are some additional factors to consider when selecting a wedding date:

- **The Weather:** Think about the climate in your region. Have you always dreamed of a garden ceremony with an outdoor reception? Do not choose a date (or season) that will make this dream impossible.
- **Local Events:** Call your local chamber of commerce or the chamber of commerce in the city where you will be holding your ceremony and/or reception. Check the local calendar of events against possible wedding dates. You may want to hold your reception at this great hotel in the center of town, but on that same day the city's marathon will be held. Chances are the hotel will let you do it, but think about the logistical nightmare this poses for your vendors and your guests, not to mention you and your fiancé.
- **Religious Holidays and Events:** Some religions have restrictions on performing marriage ceremonies at particular times of the year. You should investigate these possibilities, as well as any other religious holidays or events taking place at the church or synagogue that may pose a conflict. If you are not aware of these days, call the church, synagogue, or your officiant before you sign any agreements.
- **Travel Time:** Do you have many guests coming from out of town? Flights and hotel rooms during certain times of the year (holidays) are quite expensive, and maybe that dear friend or relative cannot afford the price of a plane ticket.
- **School:** If you have friends or close relatives in school, consider their school schedules. Attending a wedding near the beginning or end of the school year is particularly difficult, especially if travel is involved. Additionally, May and June weddings often conflict with graduations.

- **Work:** Do you have a busy season at work? Planning a wedding in the middle of this time may pose some problems. Do you have friends at work who will be invited to the wedding? They may not be able to attend. Will you be able to take the time off from work that you need? How favorably will your boss look upon you being absent during the busy season? How will you finalize all of the details for the wedding when you are swamped with work *until* the wedding day? Ask your fiancé the same questions. Consider your parents' schedules too.
- **Your Monthly Cycle**: There is one final factor that may influence your decision when selecting the date. No one ever mentions it, but it must be said—your period. This is the last thing any bride needs to deal with on her wedding day or on her honeymoon. If this is important to you, keep these days in mind when you schedule your wedding.

Once you have considered these factors, come up with a general time frame for choosing a date, such as from the end of September to the beginning of October. Unless a particular date holds special significance, keep an open mind. Check with your families to see if this time frame fits into their schedules.

To reserve the location and/or vendors of your choosing, you may need to compromise. Quality vendors and popular locations can be booked anywhere from one to two years ahead of time. If you really have your heart set on a special location, you may need to actually find out what dates are available. On the other hand, if you have your heart set on a specific date, you may have to look for locations or vendors that are available on that date. Yet, still, if you are choosing a popular date, like a Saturday that happens to be Valentine's Day, you may need to consider booking your location and vendors *very* early. No matter how much you prepare and plan, compromise is sometimes inevitable.

WEDDING STYLE

You may not have been dreaming of this day since you were a little girl, but now that your wedding is a reality, it is time to start. A wedding is the first opportunity to showcase all the unique qualities and characteristics you possess as a couple. Your wedding style is what the guests will first notice. It is personal, unique, and so very *you*.

While many weddings seem as though they come from the same old cookie cutter, the addition of your personal touches to the ceremony and reception will set your wedding apart from the others. When you begin planning your wedding, forget about the old "rules." If you want to add a little color to your gown, or if you want your dog to walk down the aisle with you—go for it!

Influences on Wedding Style

In many instances, lifestyle or social standing may dictate the style of a wedding. One of the most important factors to consider is in which type of setting you and your fiancé will be the most comfortable and at ease. You will also want to consider how the majority of your guests will feel. A black-tie affair for a casual crowd may not be a logical choice, nor would a casual lunch suit a society crowd.

The location you select for the ceremony and/or reception will influence the style of your wedding. The location can dictate the formality of a wedding as well as set the overall mood, as it will be the guests' first impression of the wedding festivities. Selecting a location can make the other stylistic decisions fall into place. You may choose to take certain elements from the location, such as a blooming rose garden, and build on that idea, incorporating a rose theme into your invitation ensemble, wedding programs, and favors.

While guests expect formal weddings to be held at grand hotels, country clubs, and private estates, you are not limited to these sites should you want a formal wedding. A creative, resourceful couple can hold a wedding anywhere they choose, even in a barn. As in all other decisions you make regarding your wedding, use your creativity. The "rules" for weddings today are flexible. You are not locked into anything.

The budget will affect your stylistic choices as well. Formal weddings, as a rule, require larger budgets. If you are holding your reception at a historic mansion, with all the trimmings, you cannot skimp on the rentals or serve the guests on paper plates. When you choose to have a formal wedding, you need to maintain the same level of formality throughout the wedding. Consequently, the elements that make up a formal wedding, engraved invitations, lavish floral centerpieces, and fine china place settings, will add substantial costs to your bottom line.

With a less formal wedding, you are able to get away with budgetary shortcuts, using more creativity in lieu of more money. However, it is not always about how much money you spend, but how you *choose* to spend it. There have been couples known to spend $30,000 on an all-out extravaganza for fifty guests, while others have spent $5,000 on a simple but elegant luncheon for one hundred guests.

Your interests, whether mutual or individual, can influence the style of your wedding. Many couples are choosing to showcase particular interests or hobbies by having a theme wedding. Think about the activities in which you and your fiancé like to participate. Maybe you are ballroom dancers. That is a great beginning to establish a unique look and feel for your wedding. Do you surf? Think about a wedding with a beach theme.

Even your careers can influence style. Is one of you an artist? A wedding held in an art gallery won't require much decorating, and it could be the perfect place to celebrate your love. Your wedding can be anything you want it to be—incorporate the important aspects of your life into your celebration.

If You Are Still Not Sure . . .

If you are still having difficulty conveying your ideas regarding wedding style to others, you may wish to try the following:

Make a list of descriptive words, or, if visuals work better for you, pull together pictures from bridal magazines. Go through your list of words, or narrow down your pictures, until you have three or four distinct words or images left. Use these words and visuals to establish a guideline for creating your wedding style. File the photos in your Portable Planner and show them to the appropriate vendors to convey the style and look you are hoping to achieve.

MONEY MATTERS

You are about to embark on the section of wedding planning that causes the most friction and debate—the budget. While this is not the most exciting part of planning, it is absolutely necessary. A well-thought-out budget is of the utmost importance in wedding planning—as is sticking to it.

Establishing your budget calls for some frank discussions about money. More and more, the financial responsibilities of a wedding are not falling solely on the shoulders of the bride's parents. Often, the groom's family makes a contribution. It is also not uncommon for the bride and groom to contribute to—or even pay for all of—the wedding expenses themselves.

Each and every situation is unique and should be handled as such. When and if you approach your families for a contribution, do so with tact and grace. Demanding that they help pay will get you nowhere. Approach them with some important facts in place: the approximate size, date, and style of the wedding. Ask them if they can contribute, and find out how much. You may be familiar with your family's financial situation, and if so, you should not ask for something you know they cannot afford to give.

Many families do not feel comfortable handing out large amounts of cash. If this is the case, ask them to help with specific segments of the budget. For example, you can ask your fiancé's family to pay for the florist and the photographer.

Keys to a Successful Budget

1. **Determine where the money is coming from.** You will need to know who will be contributing to the wedding finances, as well as the actual dollar amounts you can count on from these parties.
2. **Determine how much you and your fiancé can contribute up front.** Also, determine how much money you will be able to save during the period leading up to the wedding. True, paying vendors with credit cards can protect your rights, but you should try not to rely on your credit to pay for your wedding. Starting your married life deep in debt is not advisable.
3. **Determine how the money is to be dispersed.** It is wise to figure that about 50 percent of your total budget will be directed toward your reception site and catering. The other 50 percent will be divided among the other necessities: ceremony site, officiant's fee, photography, videography, attire, flowers, music, stationery, attendants' gifts, and favors. Before moving on to step #4, have a realistic idea of what the

reception costs are going to be. Always put some funds aside for miscellaneous expenses, such as tipping.

4. **Prioritize**. After determining the approximate cost of the reception, you and your fiancé need to determine which other parts of the wedding hold the most value or significance for the two of you. Using the Bride and Groom Budget Wish List on the next page, rank in order of importance and in dollar amounts what aspects of the wedding are most important to each of you. From here, you can play with the figures and determine how to divide the remaining money in the budget. For example, if flowers are of the utmost importance to you, but live musical entertainment is not, put the extra money toward the florist, and hire a disc jockey rather than a band.

THE BRIDE AND GROOM BUDGET WISH LIST

Subtract the estimated reception cost from the estimated total budget to determine the amount of money remaining in the budget. Then, using the directions from #4 in Keys to a Successful Budget (above), number the following from most important to least important, and include estimated dollar amounts under the $ column.

$_____   Estimated Total Budget

$_____   Estimated Reception Cost

$_____   Remaining Budget

BRIDE'S WISH LIST	RANK	$
Attire	____	_____
Bridal Beauty	____	_____
Ceremony	____	_____

GROOM'S WISH LIST	RANK	$
Material	____	_____
Bridal Beauty	____	_____
Ceremony	____	_____

BRIDE'S WISH LIST

	RANK	$
Flowers	____	_____
Honeymoon	____	_____
Musical Entertainment	____	_____
Photography	____	_____
Rehearsal Dinner	____	_____
Stationery	____	_____
Transportation	____	_____
Videography	____	_____
Wedding Cake	____	_____
Wedding Consultant	____	_____
Wedding Rings	____	_____
Miscellaneous	____	_____

GROOM'S WISH LIST

	RANK	$
Flowers	____	_____
Honeymoon	____	_____
Musical Entertainment	____	_____
Photography	____	_____
Rehearsal Dinner	____	_____
Stationery	____	_____
Transportation	____	_____
Videography	____	_____
Wedding Cake	____	_____
Wedding Consultant	____	_____
Wedding Rings	____	_____
Miscellaneous	____	_____

COMPLETING THE BUDGET WORKSHEET

After using the Keys to a Successful Budget and the Bride and Groom Budget Wish List (see pages 25 and 26), come to an agreement on where and how the wedding funds are actually going to be dispersed. Once you and your fiancé have done this, begin filling in the Budget Worksheet below. This worksheet will provide you with an overall picture of the budget. It will be easy to see how much you have spent and where you spent it.

Use the following steps for completing the Budget Worksheet:

1. Estimate the amount of dollars for each particular category listed, and enter this information on the worksheet under the "estimate" column.
2. Once you hire a vendor and have settled on a price, enter this amount under the "actual" column.
3. Enter the amount of deposit you give to each vendor under the "deposit" column.
4. Calculate what your outstanding balance is, and write it down under the "balance" column.
5. Under the "due date" column, enter the date your final payment is due.
6. At the end of each section is a "**TOTAL**" line. Follow the columns down, and total the amounts for a quick and easy budgetary reference.

THE BUDGET WORKSHEET

Estimated Budget: _____

	Estimate	Actual	Deposit	Balance	Due Date
ATTIRE					
BRIDE:					
Gown	$_____	$_____	$_____	$_____	_____
Veil/Headpiece	$_____	$_____	$_____	$_____	_____

	Estimate	Actual	Deposit	Balance	Due Date
Lingerie/ Hosiery	$_____	$_____	$_____	$_____	_____
Shoes	$_____	$_____	$_____	$_____	_____
Jewelry	$_____	$_____	$_____	$_____	_____
Gown Preservation	$_____	$_____	$_____	$_____	_____
Misc.	$_____	$_____	$_____	$_____	_____
GROOM:					
Tuxedo	$_____	$_____	$_____	$_____	_____
Shoes	$_____	$_____	$_____	$_____	_____
Accessories	$_____	$_____	$_____	$_____	_____
Misc.	$_____	$_____	$_____	$_____	_____
TOTAL	$_____	$_____	$_____	$_____	_____
BRIDAL BEAUTY					
Hair Stylist	$_____	$_____	$_____	$_____	_____
Makeup Artist	$_____	$_____	$_____	$_____	_____
Misc.	$_____	$_____	$_____	$_____	_____
TOTAL	$_____	$_____	$_____	$_____	_____
CEREMONY					
Officiant Fee / Donation	$_____	$_____	$_____	$_____	_____
Site Rental Fee	$_____	$_____	$_____	$_____	_____
Additional Security Deposit	$_____	$_____	$_____	$_____	_____

THE BUDGET WORKSHEET (CONT'D)

	Estimate	Actual	Deposit	Balance	Due Date
Misc.	$_____	$_____	$_____	$_____	_____
TOTAL	$_____	$_____	$_____	$_____	_____

FLOWERS

	Estimate	Actual	Deposit	Balance	Due Date
Personal Flowers	$_____	$_____	$_____	$_____	_____
Ceremony	$_____	$_____	$_____	$_____	_____
Reception	$_____	$_____	$_____	$_____	_____
Bouquet Preservation	$_____	$_____	$_____	$_____	_____
TOTAL	$_____	$_____	$_____	$_____	_____

HONEYMOON

	Estimate	Actual	Deposit	Balance	Due Date
Transportation	$_____	$_____	$_____	$_____	_____
Accommodations	$_____	$_____	$_____	$_____	_____
Daily Funds	$_____	$_____	$_____	$_____	_____
TOTAL	$_____	$_____	$_____	$_____	_____

MUSICAL ENTERTAINMENT

	Estimate	Actual	Deposit	Balance	Due Date
Ceremony	$_____	$_____	$_____	$_____	_____
Reception	$_____	$_____	$_____	$_____	_____
TOTAL	$_____	$_____	$_____	$_____	_____

PHOTOGRAPHY

	Estimate	Actual	Deposit	Balance	Due Date
Engagement Photos	$_____	$_____	$_____	$_____	_____
Formal Portrait Session	$_____	$_____	$_____	$_____	_____

	Estimate	Actual	Deposit	Balance	Due Date
Wedding Day	$_____	$_____	$_____	$_____	_____
TOTAL	$_____	$_____	$_____	$_____	_____

RECEPTION (ON-SITE CATERING)

	Estimate	Actual	Deposit	Balance	Due Date
Site Rental Fee	$_____	$_____	$_____	$_____	_____
Additional Security Deposit	$_____	$_____	$_____	$_____	_____
Meal Price	$_____	$_____	$_____	$_____	_____
Bar	$_____	$_____	$_____	$_____	_____
Cake	$_____	$_____	$_____	$_____	_____
Champagne Toast	$_____	$_____	$_____	$_____	_____
Gratuity	$_____	$_____	$_____	$_____	_____
Tax	$_____	$_____	$_____	$_____	_____
Misc.	$_____	$_____	$_____	$_____	_____
TOTAL	$_____	$_____	$_____	$_____	_____

RECEPTION (OFF-SITE CATERING)

	Estimate	Actual	Deposit	Balance	Due Date
All of the Above	$_____	$_____	$_____	$_____	_____
Service Personnel	$_____	$_____	$_____	$_____	_____
Rentals	$_____	$_____	$_____	$_____	_____
TOTAL	$_____	$_____	$_____	$_____	_____

REHEARSAL DINNER

	$_____	$_____	$_____	$_____	_____

STATIONERY

Invitations Ensemble	$_____	$_____	$_____	$_____	_____

THE BUDGET WORKSHEET (CONT'D)

	Estimate	Actual	Deposit	Balance	Due Date

(Invitation, inner/outer envelopes, reception card, reply card, reply envelope)

	Estimate	Actual	Deposit	Balance	Due Date
Announcements (Including envelope)	$_____	$_____	$_____	$_____	_____
At Home/ Name Cards	$_____	$_____	$_____	$_____	_____
Thank-You/ Informal Cards	$_____	$_____	$_____	$_____	_____
Map/ Direction Cards	$_____	$_____	$_____	$_____	_____
Pew Cards	$_____	$_____	$_____	$_____	_____
Postage (Invitations, thank-you cards, announcements)	$_____	$_____	$_____	$_____	_____
TOTAL	$_____	$_____	$_____	$_____	_____
TRANSPORTATION	$_____	$_____	$_____	$_____	_____
Limousine/ Carriage/Etc.	$_____	$_____	$_____	$_____	_____
Valet Parking	$_____	$_____	$_____	$_____	_____
TOTAL	$_____	$_____	$_____	$_____	_____
VIDEOGRAPHY	$_____	$_____	$_____	$_____	_____
WEDDING CONSULTANT	$_____	$_____	$_____	$_____	_____
WEDDING RINGS	$_____	$_____	$_____	$_____	_____

	Estimate	Actual	Deposit	Balance	Due Date
MISCELLANEOUS					
Gifts (Wedding Party, Family)	$_____	$_____	$_____	$_____	_____
Disposable Cameras/Film	$_____	$_____	$_____	$_____	_____
Wedding Night Hotel Room	$_____	$_____	$_____	$_____	_____
Favors	$_____	$_____	$_____	$_____	_____
Tips for Vendors	$_____	$_____	$_____	$_____	_____
Accessories	$_____	$_____	$_____	$_____	_____

(Toasting Goblets, Guest Book, Ring Pillow,
Cake Knife and Server, etc.)

	Estimate	Actual	Deposit	Balance	Due Date
OTHER					
	$_____	$_____	$_____	$_____	_____
	$_____	$_____	$_____	$_____	_____
TOTAL	$_____	$_____	$_____	$_____	_____
Grand Total	$_____	$_____	$_____	$_____	_____

4

Creative Planning

Chances are you and your fiancé are working full time, as well as maintaining a full social calendar. The few moments of free time that still exist in your life should be put to the best possible use. By now you have used a portion of that time to do some wedding-related research and establish an organizational system. Still, you may be wondering, "How am I going to manage all this?" With a little creativity, the answer is not too far away.

It is amazing how much you can accomplish in even a few moments. The following chapter outlines some tips for doing just that. And if you are still feeling overwhelmed, now is when you need to remember that you are not alone in this venture; you have a groom, a wedding party, and a family to look to for assistance. And if you still need a little extra boost, a wedding consultant may be just the answer. Planning your wedding should be an enjoyable part of your life, not take it over.

MAKING WEDDING PLANS AT WORK WITHOUT GETTING IN TROUBLE

Like most busy professionals, you probably spend a large part of your day at the office or on the road. Learning to take advantage of the planning possibilities right in front of you will ease the load. Yet, while planning your wedding is important to you, and you can get caught up in the excitement, by all means, remember your job is your first priority, and you should do nothing to jeopardize your employment. The following are some ideas for fitting wedding planning into your busy work schedule:

- **Utilize your lunch hour.** Meet with vendors, run wedding-related errands, and fill out paperwork.
- **Fax it!** Floor plans, menu ideas, and price quotes from vendors can all be dealt with via your office fax.
- **Use your breaks.** E-mail family members, the wedding party, and vendors with new wedding information. You can also make quick phone calls and "surf the net."
- **Drive time.** Pop in DJ or band demo tapes while you commute. If you have a cellular phone, you can schedule appointments, ask questions, and pass along information to interested parties.

DO YOU NEED A WEDDING CONSULTANT?

With so many couples marrying later in life, holding down full-time jobs, and maintaining a complex social schedule, a wedding consultant is often well worth the money she costs. While such services were once reserved for the wealthy, today's brides and grooms with budgets both large and small are benefiting from these services.

"What exactly can a wedding consultant do for me?" you may wonder. A wedding consultant will be able to guide you through the planning, as well as offer advice and wisdom in all wedding-related matters. Her assets include being a planner, an organizer, an advisor, and a negotiator, just to name a few. Her most basic duties are to plan, coordinate, and direct your wedding. Yet each bride requires something different for her wedding, and wedding consultants are usually more than happy to personalize their services to accommodate individual needs.

One important aspect to keep in mind is that most churches and reception venues have a site coordinator. These positions are not the same as a wedding consultant. The church wedding coordinator is there to see that the rules of the church are followed and to act on behalf of the church. The reception site coordinator is employed by the site and is there to act on its behalf. On the other hand, when you hire a wedding consultant, you pay her fee, and she is there to act for your best interests.

Services

The following is a list of basic services most wedding consultants offer:

- Help you set up a budget tailored to your needs and desires. She will also help you stick to that budget.
- Recommend and accompany you when looking for ceremony and reception locations.
- Recommend quality, trustworthy vendors and accompany you to the meetings.
- Negotiate prices and packages with the vendors.
- Review contracts.
- Act as your representative.
- Prepare and send out vendor confirmation letters two to three weeks before the wedding date.
- Work with you and the officiant to prepare an itinerary for the rehearsal.
- Direct the rehearsal.
- Work with you and the vendors to prepare an itinerary for the ceremony and reception.
- Coordinate and supervise all details for the ceremony and reception.

- Be the point person on the wedding day. The consultant, through her years of experience, is able to foresee problems and head them off. She is prepared to handle unexpected situations and minor disasters, and to solve them quickly.

Benefits

Brides have been planning their own weddings for years, and by all means so can you. However, the demanding personal and professional commitments of today's brides and grooms do not always allow a bride to give her full attention to wedding planning. Outlined below are some of the additional benefits of hiring a wedding consultant:

- A consultant is familiar with a vendor's work, demeanor, and style. She will be able to direct you to a vendor who is a good match for your style and personality. The consultant is also familiar with the prices, services, and/or packages each vendor offers.
- The consultant may be able to pass along discounts to you, as vendors may pass these along to the consultant for bringing clients to them time after time.
- The consultant can advise you on all wedding-related matters, such as attire for yourself, the groom, the wedding party, and family members.
- She knows proper wedding etiquette, and is current on the trends and evolving twists to traditional etiquette.
- If you are planning a destination or long-distance wedding, a wedding consultant in that particular area can keep things in order for you in your absence. She is acquainted with that area and can refer you to vendors, as well as run small wedding-related errands. This may be reflected in her cost.
- She can act as a liaison between difficult family members, vendors, and friends, allowing you to stay out of the situation.

Fees

All this expertise and experience comes at a price. Fees for wedding consultants vary from region to region—the national average is approximately $1,500. However, there are wedding consultants available in all price levels. Keep in mind some brides spend $300 and others spend $7,000. Do not be afraid to negotiate. Many consultants will work with you to find a price that meets both of your needs.

Fees are based on a variety of factors. Some consultants will assess the amount of time they will be allotting to a particular couple, and will charge a fee according to this assessment. Others charge a flat fee, regardless of the couple's budget. Still others charge anywhere from 10 to 15 percent of the total wedding budget.

In many instances, wedding consultants will also give the bride the opportunity to pay an hourly fee, charging as a lawyer would, based upon the amount of time devoted to that wedding. They may also break down their services into separate categories, such as charging $200 to plan and direct the rehearsal, while assessing an additional $800 fee to do the same on the actual wedding day.

Interviewing and Hiring a Consultant

The profession of wedding consultants is not regulated. In most states, there is no specific training one must have to call herself a wedding consultant. Therefore, it is a situation of "bride beware." Check on her references, call the Better Business Bureau, thoroughly interview the consultant, and trust your instincts.

Unless you are familiar with the work of a particular wedding consultant, it is recommended to interview at least three candidates before making a final decision. During this interview, you are trying to get a sense of who they are, and how their services can benefit you. Ask to see photos of weddings they have done in the past to get a feel for their style. Request a list of brides and vendors you may call as references.

Communicate your needs and the level of consultant involvement you require at the initial meeting. A good consultant will wait for direction from the bride, offering her opinion when necessary or when asked. She will listen to your requests, and will not push you into arrangements based on her best interests or desires.

Before you begin interviewing consultants, you and your fiancé should have made some basic decisions (see Chapter Three for more details on determining some of these factors):

1. The number of guests
2. An approximate budget

3. The approximate date of the wedding
4. The approximate time of the wedding
5. The formality of the wedding

When you hire a wedding consultant, you should look for someone with expertise in, and a thorough knowledge of, the wedding industry. Often, these traits come after years of experience. While experience is often a good measure of a wedding consultant's value, it should not be the deciding factor. A less experienced wedding consultant may possess all the skills, creativity, and enthusiasm necessary to create, coordinate, and direct your wedding just as a more experienced consultant would, and possibly for a lower fee.

Should you be interested in a consultant with less experience than others, trust your instincts. If you feel comfortable with her, and she is knowledgeable, take the next step. Call her references and do some investigating. Finally, ask about her background and training. Look for a "Certified Wedding Consultant," which means she has had some formal training in this area, either under the supervision of an experienced wedding consultant or through a correspondence course. Consultants who have taken these courses have spent hours learning about the wedding business.

Personality plays an important role in this decision as well. If you are a casual and laid-back bride, a high-strung consultant is not a good match. You and the consultant should have similar tastes and styles. You should have a feeling of camaraderie and mutual respect. After all, you will be working with her for many months.

Whomever you decide to hire, it is of the utmost importance that you feel comfortable and confident in your choice. Both you and the consultant will be able to feel if there is any connection at the first meeting. If the consultant "rubs you the wrong way," or vice versa, move on to another. There are many wedding consultants willing and ready to assist you in planning your special day.

After interviewing the consultants on your list, evaluate each one by asking yourself these questions:

- Was she enthusiastic and interested in what I had to say?
- Did she listen to my ideas, concerns, and comments?
- Did she answer my questions directly and treat me with respect?

- Did her appearance, demeanor, and overall attitude reflect a positive or appropriate image?
- Is her experience appropriate for my type of wedding? For example, if you are having a traditional Jewish wedding, has the consultant had any experience with the particular customs or arrangements that are necessary for this type of celebration?
- Do her fees work into my budget? Are her fees reasonable? Are they in line with others I have interviewed?
- Was she pushy, urging me to sign a contract right away?

Once you have made a decision, sign a contract and pay your deposit, usually 50 percent of the total fee. The contract should include the date, type or extent of service to be provided, and outline any additional arrangements that were discussed and agreed upon by the two of you. Remember that the date may be affected by the availability of the ceremony or reception location. Bring this up with the consultant if you have not yet decided on a location.

THE ROLE OF THE WEDDING PARTY

Choosing a wedding party is about more than who looks good in a pink taffeta dress or a rented tuxedo. It is about you and your fiancé honoring special friends, relatives, and siblings, and about them honoring you. The wedding party is there to assist with wedding-related matters and lend support throughout the planning, and especially on the wedding day. A good wedding party is part of the team that helps your wedding run smoothly.

While many see the role of the wedding party as largely ceremonial, in actuality they are there to help you. Hopefully they understood this commitment when they accepted your invitation to be a member of the wedding party. Even so, when and if you ask them to assist you with a particular task, do not demand; ask nicely, and if they are not comfortable with a particular task, ask if there is something else they would feel more comfortable doing.

Once you have found some special people who are willing to pitch in and help you get your plans off the ground, make copies of the Bride "In Need"

Task Sheet (see page 48). Then, fill out each sheet individually and distribute them to the appropriate people.

The following is a partial list of tasks with which the wedding party may be able to assist. Keep the limitations of each person in mind when delegating duties.

- Host a bridal or co-ed shower.
- Throw a bachelor/bachelorette party.
- Shop with the bride for bridesmaids' dresses. (Take only one attendant.)
- Shop with the bride for wedding gown. (Take only one attendant.)
- Help make wedding favors.
- Help assemble or make wedding programs.
- Help address and assemble invitations.
- Research accommodations for out-of-town guests.
- Refer you to trustworthy vendors.
- Prepare the Wedding Day Tool Kit (see page 212).
- Help make wedding accessories, such as the ring pillow, flower girl basket, or table centerpieces.
- Help prepare "confirmation packages" for the vendors, wedding party, and family members (see page 203).
- Listen to you while you are going through this crazy but wonderful time in your life.

Selecting the Wedding Party

The selection of a wedding party is not limited by the "rules" of weddings past. Today, just as you will tailor your wedding to fit your needs, you can choose a wedding party that is truly representative of your interests and lifestyle. Foremost, the number of bridesmaids and groomsmen do not need to be even. Do not feel obligated to ask someone you don't really want to be part of the wedding party, or ask someone for the sake of making the sides equal. There are ways to work around this during the processional and recessional. Consult with your officiant or consultant for ways to make this situation work.

At the very least, you will need to select a Maid/Matron of Honor and a Best Man. These are the two designated witnesses at the ceremony, and will sign the marriage license as such. Because of this, they should be of legal age to sign an official document. If you'd like, you may choose to have two Maids/Matrons of Honor or Best Men.

Once you have selected the Maid/Matron of Honor and the Best Man, you should select the other members (if any) of the wedding party. The members of the wedding party can include close friends, family members of the bride, or family members of the groom. The size of the wedding party should reflect the size of the wedding. For instance, a twenty-person wedding party at a wedding with seventy-five guests would seem out of place.

Depending on the size of the wedding, you may also need to select additional ushers. As a general rule, there should be at least one usher for every fifty people. Groomsmen, with the exception of the Best Man, may act as ushers, or ushers can assume additional positions. If you must select additional ushers, they need not stand up with you at the ceremony. They should, however, be recognized in the wedding program, or with a small token of your appreciation. Depending on the formality of your wedding, ushers may wear a tuxedo or an appropriate suit.

A new twist is the addition of mixed wedding parties. It is not uncommon to find a "Man of Honor" or a "groomswoman" in modern weddings. Gender no longer dictates on what side one must stand. Should this situation arise, it is appropriate to choose the proper attire. Men in the bride's entourage should wear a tuxedo. You may wish to differentiate the bride's side from the groom's by choosing different accessories (vest, cummerbund, or bow tie). A woman in the groom's entourage has two options. She may choose to wear a tuxedo or a black (or whatever color the groomsmen's tuxedos are) dress similar in style to the bridesmaids' dresses. This will depend on her style, as well as what appeals to you.

Additional members of the wedding party may include a flower girl(s), a ring bearer, and a junior bridesmaid. Flower girls should be between the ages of four and eight, junior bridesmaids from nine to fourteen, and ring bearers from four to ten years of age. You may wish to include a position of "junior groomsman" for boys who are too old for the ring bearer position and too young to be a groomsman or usher.

The wedding party is expected to pay for their own attire, shoes, and accessories, as well as travel arrangements. The bride and groom should provide the bouquets or boutonnieres, and thank them with an appropriate gift, usually at the rehearsal dinner. Use the Wedding Party Roster (see page 49) to keep track of addresses, phone numbers, E-mail addresses, and dress, tuxedo, and shoe sizes.

GET A LITTLE HELP FROM YOUR GROOM, FAMILY, AND FRIENDS

Brides often get caught up in the planning, taking on all the responsibility themselves. A wise bride knows now is the time to delegate. It often takes some coaxing to get the groom involved in the planning, so be creative in the tasks in which you include him. The families are often all too willing to help out, so set aside a few tasks for them. And finally, utilize the services and talents of your friends. With a little creative "team management," you will be able to relax a little and still accomplish all the necessary tasks.

The Groom

Do what you can to get the groom involved; after all, it's his wedding too. It may take a little more creativity and imagination to come up with some "groom friendly" tasks, but it is all worth it in the end. The following are some responsibilities the groom can take on depending on his capabilities and interests:

- Prepare his guest list and have his family prepare theirs. Order the list from "most necessary" to "least necessary" to invite (see page 62).
- Collect the addresses for his guest list, and for those on his family's guest list.
- Select his Best Man and wedding party.
- Shop for and select formal wear for himself and his wedding party.
- Sample cakes, pastries, wines, champagnes, and menu selections.
- Accompany you on visits to ceremony/reception sites.
- Meet with officiant and map out details with him, especially if you will be marrying at his family's church.
- Help assemble invitations.
- Listen to audiocassettes from bands or DJs.

- View demo tapes from videographers.
- Make maps for the rehearsal, ceremony, and reception locations.
- Develop your own wedding web site.
- Help out with other computer "stuff"—make menu cards, wedding programs, etc.
- Help prepare and assemble "confirmation packages" for vendors, wedding party, and family members (see page 203).
- Track the budget.
- Research and make honeymoon plans.
- Research requirements for obtaining a marriage license within the appropriate state or county, and make sure both of you have all the necessary paperwork—birth certificate, blood test, proof of divorce, proof of citizenship, etc. (see page 178).
- Obtain or upgrade insurance policies for your new home and life together.
- Be responsible for seeing that the marriage license is signed and mailed in before you leave for the honeymoon.

The Families

Involving family members is a nice way of inviting them to share in a special part of the wedding planning. They are often eager to help out. Yet, while you may not want to relinquish some of the more stylistic duties or involve them in the crucial decision making, there are quite a few tasks with which they can assist you.

- Research possibilities for wedding favors.
- Meet with the church officiant, especially if it is the family's church.
- Assist the bride in selecting her wedding gown. (Usually the bride's mother.)
- Research centerpiece ideas, should you decide not to have the florist create them.
- Prepare a guest list, ordering the list from "most necessary" to "least necessary" to invite.
- Collect addresses for those on the guest list.

- Help make wedding accessories such as the ring pillow, flower girl basket, or table centerpieces.
- Research accommodations for the out-of-town guests.
- Help assemble invitations.
- Help prepare "confirmation packages" for vendors, wedding party, and family members (see page 203).
- Greet guests the day of the wedding.
- If a family member is a good photographer, supply him with numerous rolls of film and ask him to take candid photos throughout the festivities, including the rehearsal, rehearsal dinner, prewedding activities, and at the reception.
- Host a get-acquainted BBQ or dinner as friends and family arrive from out-of-town.
- Make arrangements for light snacks for the wedding party and families on the wedding day. Between getting your hair done, taking pictures and such, it can be a long day for everyone if you have to wait until dinner to eat.
- Mail wedding announcements the day of or the day after the wedding.
- Send out the bridal bouquet for preservation after the wedding.
- Send out the wedding gown for preservation after the wedding.

The Friends

If you have not hired a wedding consultant, ask a trustworthy friend or family member to play "Troubleshooter." On the wedding day, she will be armed with the completed Portable Planner (see page 3), the itinerary, and the cellular phone and/or pager that matches the contact number you have given the vendors. When you ask someone to do this, you should feel confident about her ability to think fast and handle responsibility. This is an extremely important "job."

Once you have decided on someone, and she has accepted, spread the word that all problems and questions should be directed to her on the wedding day. Instruct her to report to you or the groom only in extreme circumstances. Pass the name of the "Troubleshooter" along to the vendors in your "confirmation package" (see page 203). Have the vendors "check in" with her and "check out" with her before they leave the facility. The "Troubleshooter" should also attend the rehearsal to acquaint herself with the people and the locations.

Should the job of "Troubleshooter" seem overwhelming, consider the other jobs with which your friends can assist you. You may be surprised at how many people are honored to be a part of your "wedding day team."

- Ask one or two friends to be greeters at the ceremony and/or reception. They can pass out wedding programs, direct guests to sign the guest book, inform guests with children that child care is available, and assist in finishing up any last minute details. At the reception, the greeters can help direct guests to their seats.
- You may also want to ask a few friends to be in charge of the gifts. They will make sure the cards are securely attached to gifts, and ensure that the gifts are taken to the appropriate car after the reception.
- If a friend is a good photographer, supply her with numerous rolls of film and ask her to take candid photos throughout the festivities, including the rehearsal, rehearsal dinner, pre-wedding activities, and at the reception.

THE WEDDING CONSULTANT

Name of Company: _____

Consultant's Name: _____

Phone: _____ Fax: _____

E-mail: _____

Address: _____

Dates Available: _____

QUESTIONS TO ASK

- How long have you been in the business? What is your experience? Training?
- Do you work with all budgets?

- What is the usual type of wedding with which you are involved?

- What types of locations do you represent/work with on a regular basis? (A consultant who deals only with hotels may not have the experience to deal with rentals, caterers, and all the additional details that come with other types of locations.)

- Are you familiar with the particular customs of our heritage (i.e., a Jewish wedding, African-American wedding, Asian wedding)?

- What specifically will you assist us with/do for us before and on the wedding day?

- Will you organize and direct the rehearsal?

- Will you prepare itineraries for the rehearsal, ceremony, and/or reception?

- What time do you arrive on the wedding day?

- What do you wear to the wedding?

- Are your services all-inclusive or available separately?

- What are your fees? What are they based on?

- How much do you require as a down payment? When is the full payment due?

ADDITIONAL COMMENTS:

_____

_____

_____

_____

_____

_____

THE BRIDE "IN NEED" TASK SHEET

Given To: _____

Phone: _____   Fax: _____

E-mail: _____

Date: _____   Date to Be Completed: _____

Please Help Me With: _____

_____

_____

_____

_____

_____

_____

Specific Instructions/Requests/Comments: _____

_____

_____

_____

_____

_____

Thanks For Your Help. If You Have Any Questions, Contact Me At:

Home: _____   Work: _____

E-mail: _____

WEDDING PARTY ROSTER: THE BRIDE'S ENTOURAGE

MAID/MATRON OF HONOR

Name:

Address:

Phone Number: Fax Number:

Work Phone Number: Dress Size/Measurements:

E-mail: Shoe Size:

BRIDESMAIDS

Name:

Address:

Phone Number: Fax Number:

Work Phone Number: Dress Size/Measurements:

E-mail: Shoe Size:

Name:

Address:

Phone Number: Fax Number:

Work Phone Number: Dress Size/Measurements:

E-mail: Shoe Size:

Name:

Address:

Phone Number: Fax Number:

Work Phone Number: Dress Size/Measurements:

E-mail: Shoe Size:

WEDDING PARTY ROSTER: THE BRIDE'S ENTOURAGE (CONT'D)

Name:

Address:

Phone Number:	Fax Number:
Work Phone Number:	Dress Size/Measurements:
E-mail:	Shoe Size:

Name:

Address:

Phone Number:	Fax Number:
Work Phone Number:	Dress Size/Measurements:
E-mail:	Shoe Size:

Name:

Address:

Phone Number:	Fax Number:
Work Phone Number:	Dress Size/Measurements:
E-mail:	Shoe Size:

WEDDING PARTY ROSTER: THE GROOM'S ENTOURAGE

BEST MAN

Name:

Address:

Phone Number:	Fax Number:

Work Phone Number: _____ Tuxedo/Suit Size: _____

E-mail: _____ Shoe Size: _____

GROOMSMEN/USHERS

Name: _____

Address: _____

Phone Number: _____ Fax Number: _____

Work Phone Number: _____ Tuxedo/Suit Size: _____

E-mail: _____ Shoe Size: _____

Name: _____

Address: _____

Phone Number: _____ Fax Number: _____

Work Phone Number: _____ Tuxedo/Suit Size: _____

E-mail: _____ Shoe Size: _____

Name: _____

Address: _____

Phone Number: _____ Fax Number: _____

Work Phone Number: _____ Tuxedo/Suit Size: _____

E-mail: _____ Shoe Size: _____

Name: _____

Address: _____

Phone Number: _____ Fax Number: _____

Work Phone Number: _____ Tuxedo/Suit Size: _____

E-mail: _____ Shoe Size: _____

Name: _____

Address: _____

WEDDING PARTY ROSTER:
THE GROOM'S ENTOURAGE (CONT'D)

Phone Number: _____ Fax Number: _____

Work Phone Number: _____ Tuxedo/Suit Size: _____

E-mail: _____ Shoe Size: _____

Name: _____

Address: _____

Phone Number: _____ Fax Number: _____

Work Phone Number: _____ Dress Size/Measurements: _____

E-mail: _____ Shoe Size: _____

WEDDING PARTY ROSTER:
ADDITIONAL MEMBERS OF THE ENTOURAGE

JUNIOR BRIDESMAID

Name: _____

Parent's Name: _____

Address: _____

Phone Number: _____ Dress Size/Measurements: _____

E-mail: _____ Shoe Size: _____

Name: _____

Parent's Name: _____

Address: _____

Phone Number: _____ Dress Size/Measurements: _____

E-mail: _____ Shoe Size: _____

FLOWER GIRL

Name: _____

Parent's Name: _____

Address: _____

Phone Number: _____ Dress Size/Measurements: _____

E-mail: _____ Shoe Size: _____

RING BEARER

Name: _____

Parent's Name: _____

Address: _____

Phone Number: _____ Tuxedo/Suit Size: _____

E-mail: _____ Shoe Size: _____

JUNIOR GROOMSMEN

Name: _____

Parent's Name: _____

Address: _____

Phone Number: _____ Tuxedo/Suit Size: _____

E-mail: _____ Shoe Size: _____

Name: _____

Parent's Name: _____

Address: _____

WEDDING PARTY ROSTER:
ADDITIONAL MEMBERS OF THE ENTOURAGE
(CONT'D)

Phone Number: _____   Fax Number: _____

E-mail: _____   Shoe Size: _____

JUNIOR GROOMSMEN (CONT'D)

Name: _____

Parent's Name: _____

Address: _____

Phone Number: _____   Tuxedo/Suit Size: _____

E-mail: _____

ADDITIONAL COMMENTS:

_____

_____

_____

_____

_____

_____

_____

_____

_____

_____

_____

5

The Six-Weekend Wedding Planner

By this point, you and your fiancé have had the opportunity to collaborate on the perfect vision for your wedding day. As well, you have discussed how much you and your families are willing to spend to make that vision a reality. You are now ready to tackle the heart of the wedding planning process.

While you want your wedding day to be a truly spectacular celebration, you cannot afford to have your life dominated by endless meetings with caterers, florists, and the like. This is where the Six-Weekend Wedding Planner comes to the rescue. This section maps out a complete and comprehensive guide to planning this special day in your life, without having to devote your entire life to planning it.

The key to making this method work is doing your homework! Before you even begin your first weekend goal, you should have completed the preplanning steps outlined in the first section of the book. The more prepared you are, the more efficiently you will be able to accomplish all of the weekend goals. Before proceeding any further, ask yourself the following questions:

- Do we have a wedding date in mind?
- Are we organized?
- Have we done research and gathered referrals?
- Do we know how much money we can spend, and where we can spend it?
- Have we selected our wedding day team? (Have we hired a wedding consultant, chosen the wedding party, and asked friends and family for help?)

If you can answer "yes" to the above questions, you are ready to dive into the Six-Weekend Wedding Planner. You will be doing a lot of work throughout these next weeks, and to help you keep all of the information straight, you will find special worksheets at the end of each weekend section that consist of the following:

Checklists: Use the checklists throughout the book to keep track of tasks you have completed, items that need to be purchased, and things to remember. Make copies of the checklists when necessary, and distribute them to the proper people.

"Questions to Ask" Worksheets: Take these worksheets with you when you meet with vendors. Make three or four photocopies of each (one for each vendor you interview). Write their information down on these worksheets and file them in your Portable Planner (see Chapter One) after the interview. All of the questions listed may not pertain to your particular situation, so before meeting with the vendor, go through the questions and highlight the ones that are relevant to your wedding.

Keep in mind the Six-Weekend method is only a guide. In some cases, you may be able to finish the planning in less than six weekends if you are planning a smaller or more casual event, or already have particular vendors in mind. On the other hand, should you prefer to spend more time exploring florists or photographers, extend that part of the planning timeline into an additional weekend or two. Every wedding planning situation is unique, so work according to what feels most comfortable to you.

Once you have successfully navigated your way through and completed the goals laid out in the Six-Weekend Wedding Planner, your life can return to normal! Feel free to put this planner away until three weeks before the wedding. At that time, continue on to Chapter Six, where we will take you through all the final details, down the aisle, and on to your honeymoon.

HIRING VENDORS

In the next six weekends, you will be faced with making numerous decisions that will impact the final outcome of your wedding day. Among other things, you will be purchasing a bridal gown and hiring wedding day vendors. All of the vendors you select to perform a service or provide a product will ultimately contribute to the success of your wedding day. Therefore, one of the first steps in heading off wedding day disasters is to hire reputable vendors.

The following list outlines some general guidelines to follow while in the process of interviewing and hiring wedding vendors. Before you sign a single contract or put down one deposit, take the following points into account.

- Interview and get estimates from at least three vendors from each category before hiring anyone. Exceptions occur if the vendor comes highly recommended by a friend or family member, or if you have worked with him or her in the past.
- Ask each vendor you interview for references, including recent brides, and call them.
- Call the Better Business Bureau to see if there have been any complaints lodged against the vendor.
- Ask the vendors if they have the necessary business licenses and insurance.
- Use the "Questions to Ask" worksheets, at the end of each weekend section or chapter, to gather facts and get the answers to all the important questions.
- Always meet face-to-face with vendors, and see and/or hear samples of their work. If the vendor provides a tangible product, such as a florist, always ask to view a portfolio, or better yet, samples of the actual product.
- Be wary of a vendor who asks for full payment up front. Most vendors divide their payments in half, requesting half when you sign the contract and half approximately two weeks before the wedding date. The photographer will usually divide the payments in threes, one third due at the signing of the contract, one third due two weeks before the ceremony, and the remainder when you pick up your proofs or photographs.

After interviewing the vendors for a particular category, assess their skills, professionalism, and body of work. Use the following guidelines to evaluate the vendor and make an informed decision.

- Take mental note of how the vendors present themselves and their product. This is a good indication of how they do business. There are, however, vendors who do beautiful work but don't make a good presentation, either because of their personality or appearance. If their work comes highly recommended, and you can live with whatever character flaw they may have, this may not be an issue. Use your judgment.
- Ask yourself if you can work with the vendor's personality. A laid-back wedding consultant will not be a good match for a persnickety bride, or vice versa.
- What is the vendor's attitude? This is a happy time in your life, and the vendors you hire should reflect this same sentiment. They should listen to you and be ready and willing to help.
- Be aware of burnout. A photographer may have fifteen years of experience under his belt, but if he is "burned out," his equipment is outdated or in poor shape, or he is not current on new techniques; the years of experience mean nothing.

Part of putting on a successful low-stress wedding is taking responsibility yourself. It is a combination of your behavior and the vendors' that make the day a success or failure. Be a good client and keep the following points in mind.

- Periodically check in with the vendors. This doesn't mean calling to chat every week, but rather calling every other month or so. Any vendor who has been in the wedding business for a while will not be annoyed with your phone calls.
- Follow the rules of the ceremony and/or reception location. If the reception location says the festivities must end by 10:00 P.M., make sure that they do. If the room capacity is 200, don't invite 300 guests. Not following the rules can lead to the party being canceled early, and/or forfeiting your security deposit.

- Turn in any requested paperwork on time. If the DJ requests a play list two weeks before the ceremony, get it to him on time. Otherwise the DJ may not have enough time to find the special music you request. Or if you want your florist to copy a bouquet you saw in a magazine, make a color copy of the photo and get it to the florist in a timely manner—or you may not be able to get what you want.

You want your wedding day to be just what you've always imagined. Upholding your end of the contract and adhering to the above guidelines will help ensure that you are hiring the best vendors for your money, your wedding, and your lifestyle.

PROTECTING YOUR INVESTMENT

After interviewing the wedding vendors, and assessing their work using the criteria outlined throughout the book, it will be time to make your final selections. When you decide to hire any particular vendor, you will want to obtain a detailed signed contract. The contract is a crucial document designed to protect you and the vendor. Most vendors supply a standard contract, which should include the specific details for your wedding.

The following are some additional points you should remember about contracts:

- Words mean nothing. Do not assume you hired a vendor for your wedding day until all parties have signed the contract. You should always receive a copy of the contract with both signatures.
- Read the contract carefully and discuss any questions you may have. Should there be any changes, both you and the vendor should initial that particular point.
- The contract should include detailed information, including date, time, and address of the location(s), as well as the type of product or service to be provided.

- Don't forget about those hidden costs. The contract should spell out all the details, including overtime charges, delivery charges, exclusions, limitations, cancellation fees, and the refund policy.
- Include the name of the company and contact person(s) who will be working with you on the wedding day.
- If there is more than one location to which a vendor must travel, specify this and include the additional address in the contract. For example, the florist may need to deliver the personal flowers to the wedding party at the bride's parents' house, then go to the church to decorate, and then, finally, go to the reception site to decorate that location. Make sure the vendor knows this, as it may affect cost as well.
- The contract should be descriptive. For example, include the number of bouquets needed and the types of flowers, not just "bouquets for bridesmaids."

Above and beyond signing contracts to protect yourself, you may wish to consider purchasing wedding insurance. Wedding insurance starts at around $195. The type and extent of the coverage you wish to purchase will determine the exact price. Wedding insurance covers such items as postponement and cancellations, personal liability, medical payments, photographs, attire, and gifts. Wedding insurance is offered by R.V. Nuccio & Associates (call 1-800-ENGAGED for more information) and is underwritten by the Fireman's Fund Insurance Company. In the grand scheme of things, it is a small price to pay for added peace of mind.

Weekend One Checklist

☐ Create a Preliminary Guest List

☐ Secure a Location for the Ceremony

☐ Secure a Location for the Reception

☐ Hire a Caterer

☐ Obtain Additional Rental Equipment

☐ Send Out "Save the Date" Cards

CREATE A PRELIMINARY GUEST LIST

(Friday Night)

Whether you are planning an intimate gathering of your closest family and friends or a large all-out bash, creating a guest list is often one of the most difficult aspects of planning a wedding. For many couples, budget and space restrictions limit the number of guests they can invite. While this is unfortunate, it is certainly not impossible to create a reasonable guest list that includes all of the special people in your lives.

As a rule, the guest list includes close relatives, and personal and family friends. At some weddings, coworkers and business associates also make it onto the list. The bride and groom can create the guest list on their own, or, as is often the case, can accept input from each of their families. In many situations, the decisions regarding who will be included on this list are contingent upon who is financing the celebration.

Before starting your wedding guest list, it is important to establish certain guidelines ahead of time. Discuss and agree upon the following factors, as they will all greatly impact your final guest count:

- Will single guests be allowed to invite an escort to the wedding?
- Will children be welcome to attend?
- How many names will the groom be allowed to contribute to the guest list?
- How many names will the bride be allowed to contribute to the guest list?
- How many names will the bride's family be allowed to contribute to the guest list?
- How many names will the groom's family be allowed to contribute to the guest list?

Once these decisions have been made, there are a number of ways to begin compiling the guest list. One way is to divide the list into "A" and "B" categories. The "A's" are the *must* invites: your immediate families, close relatives, current close friends, members of the wedding party and their spouses, and the officiant and his spouse. The "B's" comprise the alternate list: coworkers, distant relatives, extended family, childhood friends, and maybe some college roommates you haven't been in touch with in years. Within the "A" and "B" categories, order the guests from most to least necessary to invite.

Later, during Weekend Four, when you will be finalizing the guest list, people on the "B" list can be added as space or budget allows. If names remain on the "B" list, remember that typically 10 to 20 percent of the guests you invite may not be able to attend. This factor could allow you to send invitations to people on the "B" list, as you receive regrets from those on the "A" list. To do this, you will need to have two sets of response cards printed— the second with a later "respond by" date than the first.

The number of guests at your wedding will have a greater impact on your planning than you may realize. Before you begin your search for a ceremony and a reception site, you should have a realistic estimate of the number of guests you plan to invite. The guest count could automatically rule out certain sites due to capacity or budgetary restrictions alone.

SECURE A LOCATION FOR THE CEREMONY

(Saturday and/or Sunday)

Decisions, decisions, decisions! There are so many of these that go into securing the perfect location for your wedding. One of the first is to decide what type of ceremony you wish to have. Your choices are pretty straightforward—either a religious or a civil service. After this decision is made, it becomes easier to determine exactly where you need to start your ceremony site search.

Religious ceremonies are traditionally held at a couples', or their family's, church or synagogue. If you, your future spouse, or your families are members of a church or synagogue in which you would like to be married, your first call should be to that congregation's officiant. Discuss with him the availability and requirements for getting married in that particular place of worship. If you choose, you may also want to ask him if he would be willing to perform a marriage ceremony at a nonreligious location. Many strict religious officiants will not perform a marriage ceremony outside of a church or synagogue.

For interfaith marriages (if the bride and groom come from different religious backgrounds), you will need to compromise with your fiancé when it comes to making ceremony decisions. To overcome this obstacle, many couples ask two officiants to perform—one from each faith. Most often with such an arrangement, the ceremony is held at a neutral, nonreligious location. However, with special permission and the consent of both officiants, it is sometimes possible to hold the ceremony at one or the other's place of worship.

Civil ceremonies have fewer restrictions placed upon them than their religious counterparts. When it comes to finding a nonreligious ceremony location, there are many creative alternatives to churches and synagogues. Gardens, beaches, parks, historic locations, landmarks, and private estates have all become popular sites. To find leads for these sites, consult regional bridal magazines and guides, your wedding consultant, wedding planning and resource centers, the chamber of commerce, and friends and family.

To view one of these sites, it is advisable to call the site coordinator in advance to schedule an appointment. Ask her to mail or fax you a brochure and an information packet. While you have her on the phone, also ask the following basic questions that could immediately remove the site from your list of possibilities:

- Is the site available on (fill in the date of your wedding day)?
- What is the maximum seating capacity?
- What is the approximate price?

When looking at any of these locations, it will be helpful to take along a camera or a video camera to photograph each site. After visiting a few different sites, your memories of each one may begin to blend together. The photographs or videotape you shoot will help you to keep them all straight.

Some other important factors to keep in mind when looking at ceremony locations include:

- For outdoor locations, consider the position of the sun during the time of day you will be getting married and taking photographs. Will the position of the sun make it too hot for the wedding party or any of your guests? Will the position of the sun cause unflattering shadows? If you have your heart set on a sunset ceremony, or a sunset wedding photo shoot, what time of day would work best?

- How accessible is the location by car or by foot? You may have always dreamed of having a large wedding on the top of a soaring sea cliff, but if access to it is limited, you may be forced to reconsider.
- Are there any restrictions at the site? Many public parks, for example, will not allow chairs to be set up, or allow you to reserve the location in advance of the wedding day. Can you live with such a situation?
- How far is the ceremony site from the reception sites you are considering? As a rule, the ceremony and reception sites should be no more than a thirty-minute drive from one another.

More and more couples are choosing to marry and hold their reception at the same location. This can reduce some costs and save everyone involved valuable travel time. If you are considering this option, ask any reception site coordinators with whom you meet to recommend areas within their facility that would be appropriate for holding your wedding ceremony.

Once you have decided on a site and are satisfied with the arrangements, sign a contract and put down any necessary deposits to secure it. Use the Ceremony Facility Worksheet (see page 70) to ensure that all of your important questions get answered. If you have already chosen an officiant, make certain that he also approves of this location.

SECURE A LOCATION FOR THE RECEPTION

(Saturday and/or Sunday)

Next to finding the right person to marry, finding the perfect location to hold your reception is one of the most important decisions you will make about your wedding. The reception site you choose will immediately set the stage for the festivities that follow the ceremony. It is also traditionally the largest single expense included in your wedding celebration budget.

To get your search started, use referrals from your wedding consultant, friends and family, regional bridal magazines and guides, wedding planning and resource centers, or the area's local chamber of commerce to find reception sites that interest you. Earlier in the week (or a few weeks in advance, if possible), set aside some time to call each of the site coordinators at the different locations. As you may have already done with the ceremony site coordinators, request that a brochure and an information packet be mailed or faxed to you. While you have her on the phone, ask the following basic questions that could immediately remove the site from your list of possibilities:

- Is the site available on (fill in the date of your wedding day)?
- What is the maximum seating capacity?
- What is the approximate price?

Once you have compiled a list of the sites you want to personally visit, look at a map and plan out your day. Make appointments to meet with the site coordinators to ensure that your important questions about the facility get answered. When scheduling appointments, count on spending about one hour at each location. Don't forget to allow for travel time between locations.

When you are visiting a site, take careful notes as you meet with the site coordinator and tour the facility and grounds. You may also want to bring along a camera or a video camera to photograph each site. Since you will be visiting these locations on the weekend, you will probably have the opportunity to view the facility as it is being transformed for that day's festivities—which hopefully will include a wedding or two. There will be much to consider, but let the standards you established in Chapter Three regarding the style of your wedding guide you during your search for the perfect location.

While it is important to have a wedding date already set, realize that you may have to be flexible when it comes to the availability of some of the more popular venues. The best locations are in high demand and may be booked anywhere from one to two years in advance. If you are planning a Saturday wedding, know that Saturday afternoons and evenings are usually the first dates to get booked up—and are often the most expensive days to host an event. Viable alternatives include Friday evenings, Saturday brunches or luncheons, and Sunday events.

Many reception sites such as hotels, country clubs, and restaurants are all-inclusive—meaning they have on-site caterers who you must use. They also supply tables, chairs, china, silverware, and basic table linens. This arrangement saves you the time and expense of finding a caterer and acquiring rental equipment yourself. When considering private homes or other unique locations, remember that the opposite usually holds true. With these types of locations, you will usually have the added responsibility of securing your own caterer and rental equipment.

Once you have found the perfect reception site, do not consider it yours until you have signed a contract and put down a deposit. When you sign the contract, make sure it includes the following items: the date, time, and location of the event, any meals and services included, additional costs such as corkage fees, valet or other parking fees, the number of service personnel included, and the name of the coordinator you will be working with now and on the day of the wedding (this is usually the same person). Closer to the wedding date, when all of your guests' responses are in, you will need to follow up with the reception site coordinator to confirm the number of guests attending.

HIRE A CATERER

(Saturday and/or Sunday) (Optional)

If your reception location has on-site catering available, you will not need to worry about this aspect of planning. If it does not, hiring a caterer goes hand in hand with securing your reception site. In the case of private homes, historic landmarks, and other unique locations, the services of an off-site caterer will most likely be necessary.

To find a caterer, look for advertisements in regional bridal magazines, as well as in local area yellow pages. Your wedding consultant or reception site coordinator may also be able to provide you with a list of preferred caterers. If you are calling a catering service you are unfamiliar with, ask for its references and request the opportunity to view a portfolio of pictures and/or menus of meals it has designed.

After you have done your research and have found the right caterer, you will need to set up a meeting with the person in charge of the catering service to determine the menu, and to taste the menu selections. At this time you may also want to inquire if its kitchen can accommodate any special dietary requests you may have. A good caterer will work with you to provide the most pleasing menu and the highest quality of service possible for your wedding reception. Think twice about hiring any caterer that does not take your needs and interests (as well as your budget) into consideration.

As with the reception site, you will need to sign a contract and put down a deposit for an off-site caterer. Be sure that the following details are specified in the contract: the name of the catering coordinator you will be working with; the day, time, and location of the event; the time the catering staff will arrive; food prices (per person); beverage prices (per person); specific menu choices; bartending fees (if applicable); and the number of service personnel needed. If the reception site has any special rules or restrictions, pass them along to the caterer at this time and make sure that he understands and can abide by them. About one to two weeks before the wedding date, don't forget to inform your caterer of the final guest count.

OBTAIN ADDITIONAL RENTAL EQUIPMENT

(Saturday and/or Sunday) (Optional)

For many couples, there is no need to arrange for the rental of additional equipment for their wedding. Hotels, restaurants, and country clubs almost always provide the necessary equipment for all of the wedding's festivities. Again, additional planning becomes a necessity for those holding weddings at private estates, parks, and other unique locations. With these types of sites, you are often responsible for arranging the rental of everything from lighting, to spoons, to trash cans. (For a complete list of all of the items you may need to consider renting, consult the Rental Equipment Checklist on page 79.)

Rentals may add several thousands of dollars to your bottom line. However, it can be a relatively small price to pay for the joy of having your wedding at one of these unique locations. Often your caterer will be able to refer you to a reputable rental company, and some may even handle the rentals for you as part of their package. Your wedding consultant, site coordinator, and regional bridal magazines are also good sources for referrals.

Hotel, restaurant, and country club receptions usually include the use of basic table linens in a variety of colors. But should you choose to upgrade to something more elaborate, such as lace and brocade table linens and overlays, these will need to be rented at an additional cost. Other decorative items such as columns, arches, gazebos, candelabras, potted trees, and plants are also popular rental items to help embellish any type of wedding site.

When dealing with a rental company, don't forget to get a written price quote per item, sign a contract, and put down a deposit. The total price for the rentals will not be determined until all of the response cards are in—as the guest count directly affects the number of plates, knives, chairs, and other items that you will need to rent.

SEND OUT "SAVE THE DATE" CARDS

(Sunday Evening) (Optional)

Now that some of the preliminary plans for your wedding are complete, you can effectively spread the news about your upcoming nuptials by sending out "Save the Date" cards. "Save the Date" cards are a great way to give out-of-town guests a "heads up" on any travel plans they will need to make, and will allow your family and special friends the opportunity to reserve your wedding date on their calendars.

These cards can be simple or elaborate. In their most basic form, they are rather inexpensive to send out. A postcard-size format can be created by hand or on a computer, and can then be duplicated onto card stock at a local copy store. Only postcard stamps will be required to mail them. You can, however, be as elaborate as you wish with these cards; just keep your budget in mind. If enough of your friends and family are on-line, you may consider E-mailing the news instead.

The "Save the Date" cards should only be sent to those people you are definitely planning to invite to the wedding ceremony and reception. The cards should include the following information:

- The names of the host of the wedding (optional)
- The names of the bride and groom
- The date of the wedding
- The city, state, and country (if necessary), where the wedding will take place

THE CEREMONY FACILITY WORKSHEET

Name of Location: _____

Contact's Name: _____

Site Coordinator (if different from above): _____

Phone: _____ Fax: _____

E-mail: _____

Address: _____

Dates Available: _____

FEES

Site rental fee: _____ Amount of deposit and due date: _____

Officiant's fee or donation: _____

Security or cleaning deposit: _____ How much? _____

Is it refundable? ☐ Yes ☐ No _____

Final payments due: _____ Fee for site coordinator: _____

Fee for organist: _____ Fee for soloist: _____

SPECIFICS

Time Allotment for Ceremony: _____ Room Capacity: _____

Changing Area for Bridal Party: _____

Restrictions on Music: ☐ Yes ☐ No _____

If yes, what are they? _____

Decoration Restrictions: ☐ Yes ☐ No _____

If yes, what are they? _____

QUESTIONS TO ASK

- Are there any restrictions on dates due to religious holidays?

- Do the fees include all necessary staff, or is that additional? Is tipping allowed?

- Is premarital counseling required?

- Will you marry us if one of us does not belong to that particular faith? Divorced? Of different faiths? Under what conditions?

- Will you marry us at a nonreligious site?

- Must we use the "house" musicians? Are they included in the price, or at an additional cost?

- Is the facility available for the rehearsal?

- Are photographs allowed during the ceremony? Is flash photography allowed?

- Is videotaping allowed?

- Are there restrictions on dress (no bare shoulders, yarmulkes)?

- May we write our own vows? May we have special readings or a song performed during the ceremony?

- Are there parking facilities on the property or nearby?

- Is the site wheelchair accessible?

- Is the site air-conditioned? Is the site heated?

ADDITIONAL COMMENTS:

_____

_____

_____

THE RECEPTION FACILITY WORKSHEET

(LOCATIONS WITH ON-SITE CATERING)

Name of Location: _____

Contact's Name: _____

Site Coordinator (if different from above): _____

Phone: _____ Fax: _____

E-mail: _____

Address: _____

Dates Available: _____

FEES

Site rental fee: _____

Security or cleaning deposit: _____ Is it refundable? ☐ Yes ☐ No

Gratuity/Service charge: _____ Amount of deposit: _____

Subsequent and/or final payments due: _____

Final guest count needed by: _____

SPECIFICS

Time Allotment for Event: _____ Number of events held at one time: _____

Room Capacity: _____

Number of Restrooms: _____ Location: _____

Changing Area/Room for Bridal Party: ☐ Yes ☐ No

Smoking Permitted: ☐ Yes ☐ No

Restrictions on Alcohol: ☐ Yes ☐ No   If yes, what are they?

_____

Restrictions on Amplified Music: ☐ Yes ☐ No If yes, what are they?

_____

Restrictions on Decorations: ☐ Yes ☐ No   If yes, what are they?

_____

Wall Color of Room: _____ Carpet or Floor Color: _____

Style of Chairs (color): _____

Available Linen Colors: _____

MENU OPTIONS

Hors d'oeuvres ($ per person or per piece and description): _____

_____

Buffet/Sit-Down Dinner/Lunch/Brunch ($ per person and
description): _____

_____

Beverages/Bar (options): _____

_____

ADDITIONAL COMMENTS:

_____

_____

_____

_____

_____

THE RECEPTION FACILITY WORKSHEET

(LOCATIONS WITH OFF-SITE CATERING)

Name of Location: _____

Contact's Name: _____

Site Coordinator (if different from above): _____

Phone: _____   Fax: _____

E-mail: _____

Address: _____

Dates Available: _____

FEES

Site rental fee: _____

Security or cleaning deposit: _____ Is it refundable? ☐ Yes ☐ No

Equipment rental (if necessary): _____

Gratuity/Service charge: _____   Amount of deposit: _____

Subsequent and/or final payments due: _____

Final guest count needed by: _____

SPECIFICS

Time Allotment for Event: _____   Room Capacity: _____

Number of Restrooms: _____   Location: _____

Changing Area/Room for Bridal Party: ☐ Yes ☐ No

Restrictions on Alcohol: ☐ Yes ☐ No   If yes, what are they?

Smoking Permitted: ☐ Yes ☐ No

Restrictions on Amplified Music: ☐ Yes ☐ No   If yes, what are they?

Restrictions on Decorations: ☐ Yes ☐ No   If yes, what are they?

Wall Color of Room: Carpet or Floor Color:

Style of Chairs (color):

Available Linen Colors:

QUESTIONS TO ASK

- Can the ceremony take place on the grounds as well? Where?

- Can we have the rehearsal on site? Which day?

- Specifically, what does the price include?

- Is cake cutting and service included, or is that an additional cost?

- Is a dance floor available? Is it included in the cost?

- Is there a parking fee? Is valet parking required?

- Is the necessary equipment (tables, chairs, linens, china, etc.) included, or is it an additional cost?

- Are fancy or custom-colored table linens available? At what cost?

- Does the price include set up and clean up?

- Are additional servers required for a sit-down meal? At what cost?

- How many servers will we need? Is that cost included in the price or is it additional? Are there overtime costs involved?

THE RECEPTION FACILITY WORKSHEET (CONT'D)

- Do you take credit cards? Is there a cash discount?

- What is the attire of the service personnel?

- At what time can the wedding party and other vendors begin to arrive on the wedding day?

- Do my other vendors have to be approved by you?

- Do you have referrals for other vendors?

- Do you have liability insurance? What does it cover?

- In the event of rain, what provisions are available?

- Is there any remodeling scheduled for the next six months? Year?

- Can you point out/recommend good photography locations on your grounds?

- How do you set up the room/hall/grounds for a ceremony and/or reception? May I have a floor plan?

- Are the kitchen facilities available to the caterer? Are there limitations on the caterers' use of the kitchen facilities?

- Is there a corkage fee for alcohol?

ADDITIONAL COMMENTS:

_____

_____

_____

_____

_____

_____

_____

THE CATERING WORKSHEET
(OFF-SITE CATERER)

Name of Company: _____

Contact's Name: _____

Coordinator's Name (if different from above): _____

Phone: _____   Fax: _____

E-mail: _____

Address: _____

Dates Available: _____

FEES

Equipment rental (if necessary): _____

Number and description of service personnel needed
and cost (per person/per hour): _____

Servers: _____   Chef: _____

Bartender/s: _____   Additional help: _____

Overtime charges (per hour/per person): _____

Gratuity/Service charge: _____   Amount of deposit: ___

Subsequent and/or final payments due: _____

Final guest count needed by: _____

MENU OPTIONS

Hors d'oeuvres ($ per person or per piece and description): ___

_____

Buffet/Sit-Down Dinner/Lunch/Brunch ($ per person and description):

_____

THE CATERING WORKSHEET
(OFF-SITE CATERER) (CONT'D)

Beverages/Bar (options): _____

_____

QUESTIONS TO ASK

- Are you familiar with the site? Will you adhere to their rules and restrictions?

- Specifically, what does the price include?

- Are taxes included?

- What is the price difference between a sit-down meal and a buffet?

- Does the price cover set up and clean up?

- Will you cut and serve the cake? Is that an additional fee? Will you pack the top layer of the cake for us?

- Do you operate the bar as well? What additional cost does this incur? Is there a corkage fee?

- Will you set up the rentals (tables, chairs, etc.)?

- Do you use disposable china? If we prefer, may we rent china and silverware? Is that an additional cost?

- Do you have a specialty?

- When may we taste our menu selections?

- Do you provide linens and the necessary equipment? If not, will you arrange for such items, or recommend a rental company?

- What is the staff's attire?

- Can you prepare a smaller number of meals for a special diet, such as a vegetarian plate?

- What is the deadline for menu notification and/or any changes?

- What do you do with the leftover food?
- Do you have liability insurance?
- What is your rating with the health department?
- Do you have references? May we review a portfolio of your work?

ADDITIONAL COMMENTS:

_____

_____

_____

_____

THE RENTAL EQUIPMENT CHECKLIST

(A GUIDE FOR RENTALS YOU MAY NEED TO CONSIDER.)

Name of Company: _____ Contact's Name: _____

Phone: _____ Fax: _____

E-mail: _____

Address: _____

	Quantity	Cost Each
TABLES AND CHAIRS		
☐ Cake Table	_____	_____
☐ Chairs (for the ceremony and/or reception)	_____	_____
☐ Gift Table	_____	_____
☐ Place-Card Table	_____	_____

THE RENTAL EQUIPMENT CHECKLIST (cont'd)

	Quantity	Cost Each
☐ Rectangular Table(s) for the Head Table	_____	_____
☐ Round Tables for Guests (8 or 10 persons per table)	_____	_____
☐ Tables for Food Service, Bar, DJ, etc.	_____	_____

LINENS

	Quantity	Cost Each
☐ Chair Covers	_____	_____
☐ Napkins	_____	_____
☐ Overlays	_____	_____
☐ Tablecloths	_____	_____
☐ Table Skirting	_____	_____

PLACE SETTINGS

	Quantity	Cost Each
☐ Cake/Dessert Plates	_____	_____
☐ Champagne Flutes	_____	_____
☐ Dinner China (based on 5-piece place setting)	_____	_____
☐ Forks (salad, dinner, cake)	_____	_____
☐ Hors d'Oeuvres Plates	_____	_____
☐ Knives	_____	_____
☐ Spoons	_____	_____
☐ Water Glasses	_____	_____
☐ Wineglasses	_____	_____
☐ Additional Barware	_____	_____
	_____	_____
	_____	_____
☐ Additional Serving Pieces	_____	_____
	_____	_____

MISCELLANEOUS

☐ Arches   _____   _____

☐ Candelabras   _____   _____

☐ Columns   _____   _____

☐ Dance Floor   _____   _____

☐ Garbage Cans   _____   _____

☐ Gazebo   _____   _____

☐ Lighting   _____   _____

☐ Portable Bathrooms   _____   _____

☐ Potted Trees or Plants   _____   _____

☐ Tenting   _____   _____

☐ Other   _____   _____

QUESTIONS TO ASK

- Are you familiar with the site?

- When will the rentals be dropped off?

- Do you set up the equipment? If yes, is that included in the cost? If no, where exactly do you drop off the equipment?

- When will the rentals be picked up?

- Do you have a package, or are the pieces priced individually? What is the price breakdown per piece?

- When do you need a final count for rental items?

- Do you have unique or fancy linens to choose from?

- Is a deposit required? If yes, when?

- Do you require an additional security deposit?

- When and how is final payment due?

ADDITIONAL COMMENTS:

_____

_____

_____

_____

_____

_____

_____

_____

_____

_____

_____

_____

_____

_____

_____

_____

_____

_____

_____

_____

_____

_____

_____

_____

_____

Weekend Two Checklist

☐ Select the Groom's Attire

☐ Outfit the Groom's Entourage

☐ Select the Bride's Attire

☐ Outfit the Bride's Entourage

☐ Hire a Professional Photographer

☐ Hire a Videographer

SELECT
THE GROOM'S ATTIRE

(Friday Night)

Deciding what your fiancé will wear on the "big day" may be one of the easiest steps along the road to planning the perfect wedding. The simplest scenario would be if your fiancé already owns a tuxedo, or is in the military and has a formal dress uniform that would be appropriate for the occasion. If this is the case, the only preparations you may need to make include obtaining any necessary alterations, purchasing additional accessories such as a tie, cuff links, vest, shoes, or socks, or taking the wardrobe to get professionally cleaned. If the above fits your situation, your groom is all ready to go! You can skip ahead to the next section, Outfit the Groom's Entourage.

Most grooms, however, find it necessary to purchase or rent a tuxedo. If your fiancé plans on attending many black-tie social or business events in the future, it may be more economical to purchase a tuxedo. If not, the best route would be to rent a tuxedo from a reputable tuxedo shop.

Before heading out to tuxedo shops, you should plan on giving them a call earlier in the week to find out the following information:

- How late are they open on Friday nights?
- Are appointments required or recommended?
- What is the general price range for their tuxedo and shoe rentals or purchases?
- Do they offer any special discounts for multiple rentals or purchases? (If other members of the wedding party rent or purchase tuxedos from their shop, will they reduce the rate of the groom's tuxedo rental or purchase?)
- Are they affiliated with any stores in other cities or states? (This is particularly important if you are getting married in a city far away from where you live or work. If the shop has affiliates, you can make your tuxedo selections at the shop closest to where you live, and actually pick up and drop off the tuxedo rentals at the store most convenient to the wedding site.)

By this point in time you should have already decided on the location of the wedding, the time of day, and the type of marriage ceremony that will be performed. When at the tuxedo store, let these factors, as well as the decisions you made on the style and formality of the wedding (see Chapter Three) guide you and your fiancé when selecting the perfect tuxedo.

You can save valuable time by doing your homework before you even set foot in the tuxedo shop. Look through bridal magazines or brochures for pictures of different styles of tuxedos, and select a few that you and your fiancé both consider possibilities. Show these photos to the tuxedo salesperson and this will cut down on the amount of time your fiancé will have to spend selecting and trying on different styles. If your fiancé already has a pair of dress shoes that he plans to wear to the wedding, have him bring them along to the store to wear while trying on the different outfits.

If you want your wedding to have a little pizzazz, be bold and select a nontraditional tuxedo style. Many of today's tuxedo manufacturers have designed modern variations of the traditional tuxedo jacket, shirt, and tie. These days there are many more options available from which men can choose. Have fun with the different colors and patterns of vests, ties, socks, handkerchiefs, and cummerbunds. Your wedding day should be unique, so let the groom pick the wardrobe that best suits his personality.

OUTFIT THE GROOM'S ENTOURAGE

(Friday Night)

Now that the groom's formal wear is selected, outfitting the other male members of the wedding party should be fairly simple. In most cases your groomsmen will not have their own tuxedos (and matching ones at that). Arranging tuxedo rentals for them simply requires that you and your fiancé register how many tuxedos you need, the style, and the color choices at the tuxedo shop of your choice. The groomsmen will typically take care of the remaining details, including submitting their measurements, paying any rental fees, and picking up and dropping off the tuxedos.

The groomsmen usually wear the same or a similar tuxedo as the groom, differentiating themselves with a different color tie, handkerchief, vest, or other accessory. These accessories are usually coordinated with the dress colors selected for the bride's attendants. Again, don't be afraid to let your personal styles show through and be creative in the selections you make.

Once you have registered the tuxedo selections, be sure to inform your wedding party members of the pertinent details including:

- When and where their tuxedo measurements are due
- How much the tuxedo rental will cost (unless you are planning on covering the cost for them), and when the payment is due
- If they will be expected to rent tuxedo shoes (or if they can wear their own dress shoes)
- What type of socks they will need to wear
- When and where they are expected to try on and pick up their tuxedo. Decide in advance whether you want everyone to meet at the tuxedo shop, or if one representative will pick up all the tuxedos and distribute them at a more convenient time and location. If you choose the latter, be sure to do this well before the wedding ceremony so there is enough time for any changes or alterations to be made.
- When and where they need to return the tuxedo (unless you are planning on appointing one person to collect and return all of them)

Before heading out to the tuxedo shop, it may be helpful for you and your fiancé to find out if any other family members (the father of the bride, the father of the groom, any grandfathers, etc.) would like for you to arrange tuxedo rentals for them as well. You wouldn't want to leave anyone out!

SELECT THE BRIDE'S ATTIRE

(Saturday Morning)

For many brides, the wedding gown is the single most important, as well as most expensive, item of clothing she will ever purchase. Many women have had visions of the perfect wedding dress since the time they were little girls. Others have spotted "the dress" in the pages of a bridal magazine or while at a bridal salon. Some choose to design their own dream dress. Still others have always envisioned wearing their mother's or grandmother's wedding dress when it is their turn to walk down the aisle.

When it comes to selecting this most precious garment, today's brides have a number of options. Whichever you choose, the following information will help guide you along the way.

Bridal Salons: The most popular option for brides in search of the perfect wedding dress is to visit a bridal salon. Salons carry a large number of dresses from different manufacturers, showcase the latest bridal trends, and have the largest number of dress styles available for you to try on. An additional advantage of patronizing a salon is having knowledgeable bridal consultants who provide personalized service as you search for the right dress.

The following are a few helpful hints to make the bridal salon experience more productive and enjoyable:

- Go to your appointment with photographs and magazine advertisements of dresses that appeal to you. The bridal consultant can use this information to help select gowns for you to try on.
- When trying on dresses, don't feel discouraged if the salon does not have one for you to try on in your exact size. Most salons stock their showrooms only with "sample sizes." However, the bridal consultants are trained at ingeniously clipping, strapping, and pouffing the dresses in just the right way, to make the sample-size dresses appear as though they actually fit you.
- Try on veils and headpieces while you are at the salon to determine what styles work best with the different dresses. It can be a challenge to accessorize later on when you don't have the main ingredient of your wedding ensemble—the dress—available for you to try on.

Heirloom Dresses: A more sentimental option for obtaining your wedding gown would be to wear a dress from a family member or close friend. Heirloom dresses are gaining in popularity as more and more brides find it important to walk down the aisle wearing a piece of their family history. The sentimentality attached to this dress makes it a one-of-a-kind, and you would not want to entrust it to just anyone. Should you decide to go this route, heed the following advice:

- If the dress is in disrepair or in a size much larger or smaller than your own, the cost of altering, updating, and/or restoring the dress can dramatically raise the price. Visit a dressmaker and get a written estimate of the total cost before proceeding.
- Use a dressmaker who comes highly recommended or has been in the business of altering and/or designing wedding gowns for a substantial amount of time. If the dress has extensive beading or lace work, you will want to be sure that your dressmaker has expertise with these kinds of applications as well.

Custom-Made Dresses: A good dressmaker can create a truly spectacular wedding gown from scratch using a photograph in a bridal magazine, a design of your own, a purchased pattern, or a combination of the above. Depending on the type of fabric and labor involved, this option could save you money, especially if the dress you want (from the salon) comes with a top designer's name on the label. Take the following into account when considering this option:

- A dressmaker can usually complete the dress in as much or even less time than it takes to get one delivered from a dress manufacturer.
- She can incorporate fabric, lace, or beading from an heirloom wedding dress into your new design, which is a great option for brides who want a contemporary-style dress but still want to wear a bit of their family history.
- You will not have the opportunity to try the dress on until it is completed (or almost completed). To be safe, you may want to try dresses on at a salon before deciding to go this route to see which styles best suit your body type.
- Unless you are already familiar with the dressmaker's work, you could be disappointed by how she translates your drawings or photographs into the finished product. Always check dressmakers' references and scrutinize their work if you have never used them before.

Bridal Discounters: If you are on a tight budget, or just don't feel justified spending the amount of money some salons are asking for their gowns, you may consider ordering from a bridal gown discounter. Most of the time, their gowns are not the "latest styles." However, some discounters may be able to order you the same gown that you tried on at a bridal salon. While some brides save hundreds of dollars using a discounter, others save as little as fifty. Keep the following points in mind when using a discounter:

- If you can find a dress at a bridal discounter, you will save money, but you typically lose the one-on-one service and expertise that is available at a bridal salon.
- If the dress you purchase is available "off the rack," before taking the dress home, check it over for any flaws, stains, or tears, as several people may have already tried it on before you discovered it. Most discounters do not accept returns should you discover a problem with the dress later on.

Department/Specialty Stores: You may be able to find a dress at a department store or specialty shop that you would like to wear as your wedding dress. If this is the case, you are in luck. You can purchase the dress right "off the rack" and take it home that very day. In many cases this is a big money and time saver. If you do find such a dress, keep the following in mind:

- Make sure this is "the dress." Most stores have a very strict return policy on formal dresses of any kind.
- Visit a dressmaker to get an estimate on any alterations that may need to be done.

Whichever route you choose, you will save valuable time by planning ahead (a few weeks in advance is ideal). Take care of the following items before you begin your quest for the perfect wedding dress:

- **Make an appointment:** Saturdays are typically the busiest days at bridal salons and dressmaking shops.
- **Think about who you want to accompany you:** One or two people at most work best. Make sure that they are available the day of your appointment. You don't want to elongate the process by having to make several trips to the salon or dressmaker, with different family members or friends in tow each time.
- **Wear the appropriate lingerie, and shoes if possible:** If you don't already own them, ask the salon if they provide bras and slips in your size that you can wear while trying on their dresses.

- **Bring along any bridal accessories that you already have and are definitely planning on wearing:** This could include items such as your grandmother's veil, or any special jewelry.
- **Find out if the salon or shop will allow you to photograph or videotape their dresses:** This not only makes a great memento for your scrapbook, but it also serves as a working tool for your florist, or anyone else who has a role in creating the style of your wedding.
- **Bring along your homework:** Don't forget your Portable Planner containing the photographs and drawings of potential gowns that you're interested in.
- **Determine what your budget is ahead of time:** It may be tempting, but you're only asking for heartbreak by trying on dresses you know you can't afford. Let your salesperson know your price range before you start looking.

Be sure to leave enough time between the delivery date of the dress you order and the wedding date, to take care of any alterations. If you order a dress from a bridal salon, be prepared to wait an average of six months. The salon can rush order the dress for an additional fee if you need it sooner. Some discounters have just as long of a waiting period if you order the dress from them. The time it takes a dressmaker to restore, alter, or assemble the gown from scratch will depend on the style of the dress and the amount of work that needs to be done. Obviously, if you find a dress right "off the rack," you can take it home with you the very same day.

When you place any dress order, be prepared to leave a nonrefundable deposit of as much as 50 percent of the total cost of the dress. Never pay in full unless you already have the dress in hand. Before leaving, get all the facts in writing, including the total cost, amount of deposit, additional charges (extra length, large size, etc.), dress size, style number, manufacturer, and color.

Finally, if you are considering having your wedding gown preserved after the wedding, please refer to page 237.

OUTFIT THE BRIDE'S ENTOURAGE

(Saturday Morning and/or Afternoon)

With the centerpiece of your wedding's style—the wedding dress—already in place, you can now concentrate on outfitting the remainder of your entourage. Fortunately, a bride has many choices when it comes to creating a dramatic look for her group of very special family and friends.

If time and ease are of the essence, one option for a busy bride would be to select a color scheme and then allow each one of her attendants to purchase her own gown appropriate to the occasion. If you select this method, your attendants will still maintain a unified look by wearing the same color dresses, carrying the same type of floral bouquets, and wearing matching jewelry and shoes (if you choose). They will certainly appreciate being able to select the dress that best suits them, and you will have one less detail to worry about.

This method works best if you provide your attendants with a set of guidelines including the dresses' hemline, fabric, and overall style. If you are still concerned about some of the dress choices they might make, your attendants can always try to show you the dress, or send you a photograph of it, before purchasing it. Another option along these lines is for the bride to choose a color and type of fabric, and then have each of her attendants choose her own style of dress from a variety of selections from a dressmaker or bridal salon.

By far the most traditional and popular method for outfitting the female members of the bridal party is for the bride to select matching dresses of like style and color for all of her attendants. These gowns are often purchased at a bridal salon or bridal discounter, and can also be custom-made by a dressmaker. You will save valuable travel time if you use the same vendor from which you purchased your wedding dress.

If your wedding dress supplier does not carry what you are looking for, many dresses can be found at department stores or specialty shops. The dresses found here are comparable in price, but are usually of superior quality to those sold at the bridal stores because they are designed to be worn more than just once. The catch is making sure that the store can acquire enough of the dresses in the sizes that you need. This may not always be easy, especially if you have a large number of attendants in your wedding party.

As a courtesy to the special people in your wedding party, you should try to choose a dress style that looks flattering on the majority of them, as well as a dress that is modestly priced (since traditionally your attendants pay for their own dresses). Your bridesmaids will be especially appreciative if you select a dress that they can wear again without fear of "looking like a bridesmaid."

Once you have made a decision about the dresses, be sure to inform your bridal attendants of all the pertinent details including:

- When and where their dress measurements are due. Provide them with the address and phone number of the salon, shop, or dressmaker, and the due date when the measurements (or sizes) must be turned in. You may also want to organize one specific appointment when everyone can go in together to get measured.
- How much the dress will cost. Be sure to let them know the exact amount owed, and when it is due.
- What shoes they will need to wear. Let them know if you would like them to purchase matching shoes or if they can wear their own dress shoes of appropriate style and color.
- What type of jewelry, lingerie, and hosiery they will need to wear. Let them know if they will need to purchase any of these items, or if you will be providing any of the items for them.
- When and where they are expected to try on and pick up their dress. Decide in advance whether you want everyone to meet at the dress shop, or if one representative will pick up all the dresses and distribute them at a more convenient time and location. If you choose the latter, be sure to do this well before the wedding ceremony so there is enough time for any changes or alterations to be made.

HIRE A PROFESSIONAL PHOTOGRAPHER

(Saturday Afternoon and/or Sunday)

Hiring a professional photographer will ensure that you and your fiancé, your families, and your special friends will all have wonderful photographs to enjoy from the wedding day for years to come. The main points to consider when hiring a wedding photographer are:

- The quality and style of his work
- The photographer's personality
- The cost

Before starting your search, you and your fiancé should determine what style of wedding photographer you would like to hire. Discuss the following factors to determine what photographic style you prefer:

- A skilled portrait photographer who will take mainly posed photographs
- A photojournalistic photographer who shoots more candid photographs
- An expert color photographer
- An expert black-and-white photographer
- An expert at both color and black-and-white photography
- Multiple photographers on site, shooting from different angles

The highest quality of wedding photographs available are shot using a medium-format camera and film. Medium-format film provides the greatest resolution, color, and clarity of prints, because the images are captured on a negative that is larger than the standard 35mm one. The difference in quality is most notable in prints larger than 8" x 10" in size. If, however, you are not planning on making any enlargements of your wedding photos, you may not notice the difference between medium-format and the much less expensive 35mm film.

To further determine the quality of photographers' work, study their sample wedding albums and portraits. Keep in mind that photographers only put their best work in the sample albums. If you do not like what you see in these, it would be unrealistic to expect better at your own wedding. Look for the following qualities when reviewing a photographer's work:

- How well are the shots composed?
- Are the photographs in focus?
- Does he make good use of lighting (natural and artificial)?
- Do all of the people in the photographs look good (do they look relaxed, are they smiling, are their eyes open, is everybody looking at the camera)?
- Are there a good variety of shots and different poses?

At first you may not think this is a very important consideration, but a photographer's personality plays a key role in the success of your wedding day photographs. On the wedding day, your photographer will probably spend more time with you and your new husband than any other person at your wedding. You want to be sure this person is someone you won't mind spending time with, as well as someone who will be comfortable around all of the other important people at your wedding. A photographer who has a good sense of humor, and can easily get along with you, your wedding party, family members, and guests, will be able to capture more relaxed and happy images of your wedding day. Lastly, you want to be sure that your photographer has the ability to remain unobtrusive. Your photographer should never be a distraction during any part of the ceremony or reception.

The easiest and least time-consuming route to securing a photographer would be to hire someone with whose work you are already familiar. Ask your wedding consultant, site coordinators, and especially recently married family members, friends, coworkers, and neighbors, for referrals. Take a look at your married friends' wedding albums and portraits. Ask them specific questions about what their photographer was like to work with on the wedding day, and afterward. Also, if you were pleased with the work of photographers you have hired in the past for some other purpose (such as to take graduation or family portraits), give them a call and see if they shoot weddings as well. If you need more leads, consult regional bridal magazines, or local telephone directories.

Before meeting with any photographers you should discuss the following with them:

- **Find out their availability:** You can rule out photographers automatically if they are already booked the day of your wedding.
- **Ask them to send you information:** Request a brochure, price list, and a few samples of their work to be sent to you.
- **Make an appointment to meet them:** Plan on making the appointment well in advance. Most photographers are busy shooting weddings on weekends, so weekend appointment times can be minimal during peak wedding months. You may have to schedule a midweek meeting.
- **Ask if you can view samples of their wedding albums and portraits:** Confirm that these will be available to view during your appointment time.
- **Ask for references:** If you are unfamiliar with the photographer's work, you may want to check a few of their references before taking the time to meet with them (especially if their office or studio is a great distance away from your home).

When you have finally found the perfect photographer, don't consider him hired until you have signed a contract that details the points covered during your initial meeting. Turn in any necessary deposits in a timely manner to ensure that the photographer you select is reserved for your wedding day. Good wedding photographers can get booked up fairly quickly (especially on Saturdays during high season). If you are dealing with a studio that employs several photographers, be sure that the name of the photographer you want is clearly indicated on the contract.

HIRE A VIDEOGRAPHER

(Saturday Afternoon and/or Sunday) (Optional)

Not every bride and groom decide to enlist the services of a professional videographer, but those couples who do get a lasting record of every moment of their wedding day. Couples who were either too nervous or too swept away by all of the activity on the actual day can watch the video later and experience it again with a much more relaxed state of mind. Wedding videos are also a great way of sharing the experience with family members or friends who were unable to attend. You can relive the event for many years to come, and who knows, you may even show the wedding video to your kids some day.

Before meeting with any videographers you should first discuss the following with them:

- **Find out his availability:** You can rule out a videographer automatically if he is already booked the day of your wedding.
- **Ask him to send you information:** Request a brochure, price list, and a demo tape of his work be sent to you.
- **Make an appointment to meet him:** Plan on making the appointment well in advance. Most videographers are busy shooting weddings on weekends, so weekend appointment times can be minimal during peak wedding months. You may have to schedule a midweek meeting.
- **Ask for references:** If you are unfamiliar with a videographer's work, you may want to check a few of his references before taking the time to meet with him (especially if his office is a great distance away from your home).

Many of the guidelines you use for selecting a photographer apply to hiring a videographer as well. When reviewing samples of a potential videographer's work, examine the following basic elements to determine his shooting style and quality of work:

- Are the shots in the video framed well?
- Is the video in focus?
- Is the camera work steady?
- Is all of the audio (especially during the wedding ceremony) clear and easy to hear?
- Is the editing concise, interesting, and transitional?

Just as with a photographer, the videographer's personality is an important element to take into consideration. Your videographer will be front and center during all of the important moments of your wedding day, so be sure that you can handle spending time with this person. Also, if you choose to have your videographer record taped greetings from your guests, you don't want to employ someone who will be a nuisance to your closest family and friends. The ability to "blend into the background" is an important skill for a wedding videographer to have. A videographer should never draw attention away from the bride and groom.

The easiest and least time-consuming route to securing a videographer would be to hire someone with whose work you are already familiar. Get referrals, and go with someone you already trust or someone who comes highly recommended. After all, the videographer you choose only has one opportunity to get it all on tape! If you don't have any leads, consult advertisements in regional bridal magazines for videographers in your area.

After you find a videographer you feel comfortable working with, make sure to get a written contract detailing all of the arrangements agreed upon during your meeting. Try not to delay signing the contract and turning in the necessary deposits, as good videographers get booked up quickly and will not reserve the day for you until you have given a deposit.

THE GROOM'S ATTIRE

Name of Tuxedo Shop/Tailor: _____

Name of Salesperson/Tailor: _____

Phone: _____ Fax: _____

E-mail: _____

Address: _____

Date of Appointment: _____

THE TUXEDO

Manufacturer: _____ Style Number: _____

Size Ordered: _____ Color: _____

Measurements (taken at time of ordering): _____

Price (including charges for extra length or large sizes): _____

Date Ordered: _____ Delivery Date: _____

Deposit (amount and method of payment): _____

Final Payment (due date and method of payment): _____

Pickup Date: _____ Return Date: _____

Security Deposit: _____ Is it refundable? ☐ Yes ☐ No

THE SHIRT

Manufacturer: _____ Style Number: _____

Size Ordered: _____ Color: _____ Price: _____

SHOES

Manufacturer: _____   Style Number: _____

Size Ordered: _____   Color: _____   Price: _____

ACCESSORIES

Button Covers/Cuff Links: _____

Pocket Square or Handkerchief: _____

Cummerbund/Vest/Bow Tie: _____

Manufacturer: _____   Style Number: _____

Size: _____   Color/Pattern: _____   Price: _____

THE GROOMSMEN'S ATTIRE

Name of Tuxedo Shop/Tailor: _____

Name of Salesperson/Tailor: _____

Phone: _____   Fax: _____

E-mail: _____

Address: _____

Date of Appointment: _____

THE TUXEDO

Manufacturer: _____   Style Number: _____

Color: _____

THE GROOMSMEN'S ATTIRE (CONT'D)

Name, Size Ordered, and Measurements (taken at time of ordering):

1. _____   5. _____

2. _____   6. _____

3. _____   7. _____

4. _____   8. _____

Price (including charges for extra length or large sizes): _____

Deposit: _____

Date Ordered: _____   Delivery Date: _____

Pickup Date: _____   Return Date: _____

Security Deposit: _____   Is it refundable? ☐ Yes ☐ No

THE SHIRT

Manufacturer: _____   Style Number: _____

Size: _____   Color: _____   Price: _____

SHOES

Manufacturer: _____   Style Number: _____

Size: _____   Color: _____   Price: _____

ACCESSORIES

Button Covers/Cuff Links: _____

Pocket Square or Handkerchief: _____

Cummerbund/Vest/Bow Tie: _____

Manufacturer: _____   Style Number: _____

Size: _____   Color/Pattern: _____   Price: _____

QUESTIONS TO ASK (THE TUXEDO SHOP/TAILOR)

- Where, what time, and what day can I pick up the tuxedos?

- What is your store's contingency plan in case some of the tuxedos do not fit properly? Do you keep an extra stock of this brand/style/size tuxedo in the shop?

- When is the full payment due?

- Is a damage/security deposit required? Is it refundable? Under what circumstances is it not?

- What size range of tuxedos do you carry? (This is particularly important if you need to outfit any small children, or if any of the men in the wedding party are above average weight or height.)

- When must all of the measurements for the wedding party be turned in?

- How do you prefer clients to submit measurements (in person at the store or affiliate store, by mail, by fax, by phone, etc.)?

- Do you provide measurement forms that we can send to wedding party members who live out of the area?

- Where, what time, and what day must the tuxedos be returned?

- Do all the tuxedos have to be returned to the same location? Do all the tuxedos have to be returned at the same time?

- How soon after the due date would late charges begin to apply? How much are they?

ADDITIONAL COMMENTS:

_____

_____

_____

_____

THE BRIDE'S ATTIRE

Name of Bridal Salon/Dress Shop: _____

Name of Bridal Consultant/Salesperson: _____

Phone: _____   Fax: _____

E-mail: _____

Address: _____

Date of Appointment: _____

THE GOWN

Manufacturer: _____

Style Number: _____   Color: _____

Size Ordered: _____

Measurements (taken at time of ordering): _____

Price (including charges for extra length or large sizes): _____

Date Ordered: _____   Delivery Date: _____

Deposit (amount and method of payment): _____

Final Payment (due date and method of payment): _____

Possible Alterations and Estimate of Cost: _____

HEADPIECE

Manufacturer: _____   Style Number: _____

Color: _____   Price: _____   Delivery Date: _____

VEIL

Manufacturer: _____   Style Number: _____

Color: _____   Price: _____   Delivery Date: _____

SHOES

Manufacturer: _____   Style Number: _____

Color: _____   Size: _____

Delivery Date: _____   Price: _____

LINGERIE

Bra or Other Foundation Garment: _____

Crinoline: _____

THE BRIDESMAIDS' ATTIRE

Name of Bridal Salon/Dress Shop: _____

Name of Bridal Consultant/Salesperson: _____

Phone: _____   Fax: _____

E-mail: _____

Address: _____

Date of Appointment: _____

THE DRESS

Manufacturer: _____

Style Number: _____   Color: _____

Name, Sizes Ordered, and Measurements (taken at time of ordering):

1. _____   5. _____

2. _____   6. _____

3. _____   7. _____

4. _____   8. _____

THE BRIDESMAIDS' ATTIRE (CONT'D)

Price (including charges for extra length or large sizes): _____

Date Ordered: _____   Delivery Date: _____

Deposit (amount and method of payment): _____

Final Payment (due date and method of payment): _____

SHOES

Manufacturer: _____   Style Number: _____

Color: _____   Price: _____   Delivery Date: _____

ACCESSORIES

Jewelry: _____

Hair Accessories: _____

Hosiery: _____

Gloves: _____

QUESTIONS TO ASK (THE BRIDAL SALON/DRESSMAKER)

- When will my wedding gown be ready to be picked up?

- When will my bridesmaid dresses/flower girl dresses be ready to be picked up?

- What type of guarantee can you make on the delivery date?

- Do you offer a rush service on this particular wedding gown or bridesmaid dress? If yes, how much sooner can I get the dress? At what extra cost?

- When must all of the measurements for the bridal party be turned in?

- How do you prefer clients to submit measurements (in person at the salon/shop or affiliate salon/shop, by mail, by fax, by phone, etc.)?

- Do you provide measurement forms that we can send to bridal party members who live out of the area?

- When will the final payments on the dress/dresses be due?

- Do you require a deposit? How much?

- Are alterations included? If not, at what cost could you do them? How long do they take?

- Do we have the option of getting alterations done elsewhere?

- Do you charge more for large-size dresses? Do you charge more for dresses of extra length?

- Is pressing included? If not, what do you charge for this service?

- If a slip or petticoat is required with the dress, is that included in the cost? If not, at what cost can I purchase one?

ADDITIONAL COMMENTS:

_____

_____

_____

_____

_____

_____

_____

_____

_____

_____

THE PHOTOGRAPHER

Name of Company: _____ Contact's Name: _____

Photographer's Name (if different from above): _____

Phone: _____ Fax: _____

E-mail: _____

Address: _____

Dates Available: _____

QUESTIONS TO ASK

- What type of camera do you use?

- On what format film?

- Do you shoot in color? Do you shoot in black and white? What is your specialty or preference between the two?

- What type of lenses and filters do you shoot with? What types of effects do they produce?

- What type of lighting equipment do you use?

- How would you describe your shooting style?

- What does your price include:

    How many hours of coverage?

    How many total photographs do you take?

    Do you work alone, or does your price include an assistant or any additional photographers?

    Does it include processing and printing fees?

    Does it include proofs? Can we keep the proofs? (If not, at what cost can I purchase them?)

    Does it include an album? If yes, what type?

How many and what size photographs do we get?

How many enlargements are included? If none, at what cost can I purchase enlargements?

Can we purchase the prints à la carte or must we purchase an album?

Is travel and set-up time included?

- May we purchase the negatives? At what cost?

- If we do not purchase the negatives, how long do you keep them on file? Where do you store them?

- When will the proofs be available to view?

- When will our finished prints and/or album be ready?

- What attire do you wear while shooting the wedding/ reception?

- What time can you arrive on our wedding day? How late will you stay on our wedding day?

- Are you familiar with where we are getting married?

- Are you familiar with where we are holding our reception?

- Should I send you driving instructions and a map?

- Will you honor any special requests we have as far as certain poses or group shots we wish to take?

- Will you provide us with a checklist of important shots and important people we can choose to include in the photographs? If not, can we provide you with a list?

ADDITIONAL COMMENTS:

_____

_____

_____

THE VIDEOGRAPHER

Name of Company: Contact's Name:

Videographer's Name (if different from above):

Phone: Fax:

E-mail:

Address:

Dates Available:

QUESTIONS TO ASK

- How would you describe your shooting style?

- How would you describe your editing style?

- What type of video camera do you shoot with?

- Can you provide multiple camera videography if we desire it? Can you explain the advantages and disadvantages of shooting with multiple cameras? What would you recommend for us?

- On what type of tape format will the original be shot?

- What type and how many microphones do you use in recording?

- What type of lighting equipment do you have? (This is particularly important if you are planning an evening ceremony or reception.)

- Do you need any additional equipment on site such as extension cords, electrical outlets, or indoor lighting?

- What does your price include:

  How many hours of coverage?

  Does this include editing?

What type of music and graphics will be included in the edited version of our video?

How many copies of the tape do we get and on what tape format?

Is travel and set-up time included?

- When will you guarantee delivery of the edited version of our video?

- Can we purchase the video unedited? If so, how much will you discount off the price?

- Can we have the master tapes? If not, at what cost can they be purchased?

- Will additional copies of the tape be available to purchase? At what cost?

- What attire do you wear while shooting the wedding/ reception?

- What time can you arrive on our wedding day? How late will you stay on our wedding day?

- Are you familiar with where we are getting married?

- Are you familiar with where we are having our reception?

- Should I send you driving instructions and a map?

- What type of back-up equipment do you bring along with you, in the event of any technical difficulties?

- Will you honor any special requests we may have in regard to what is shot and how it is edited?

- Will you shoot greetings from our families, wedding party, and guests on tape if we request it?

ADDITIONAL COMMENTS:

_____

_____

_____

_____

_____

_____

_____

_____

_____

_____

_____

_____

_____

_____

_____

_____

_____

_____

_____

_____

_____

_____

_____

_____

Weekend **Three** Checklist

☐ Order the Invitations

☐ Hire a Florist

☐ Hire a Baker

☐ Hire the Musical Entertainment

☐ Hire an Officiant

ORDER THE INVITATIONS

(Friday Afternoon/Evening)

The invitations that you and your fiancé send out to family members and friends will immediately set the tone for your wedding day. As soon as your guests open the envelopes, they will be able to determine the formality of the wedding, possibly the color scheme, the theme, and many other important details.

If you are planning a relatively small wedding and reception, you may decide to make your own handwritten or computer-designed invitations. However, most couples rely on the services of a professional printer or stationer for their supply of invitations. When dealing with a wedding stationer, there are several types of printing you can select from including:

- **Offset Printing:** A basic printing process that creates letters that lay flat on the paper. This type of printing is less formal than the following methods and is the least expensive.
- **Thermography:** A process that fuses ink and powder together on the paper to create raised letters that resemble engraving. This is a popular printing choice today because it has the elegance of raised print but is more affordable than engraving.
- **Engraving:** A metal plate is pressed onto the paper, causing the letters to be slightly raised. This is the most formal, traditional, and expensive printing process.

When deciding what type of printing process to select, and what type will fit into your budget, keep in mind that in addition to the actual invitations, you may also need to order outer and inner envelopes, reception cards, response cards, and response card envelopes. Some optional items you can consider ordering include printed return addresses on the outer envelopes, colored or specialized envelope linings, printed maps, and directions to the ceremony and reception site.

For consistency, you may also choose to order other accessories from the printer including thank-you notes, place cards, wedding programs, menu cards, wedding announcements, and printed napkins. For a complete list of the stationery items you need to consider purchasing, consult the Wedding Invitation Checklist (see page 121).

Before ordering anything, you will need to decide which of the above options you are willing to pay for, the exact wording you want to put on the invitations, and lastly, how many invitations you will need. The following guidelines should help you to come up with that number:

- Review your guest list and determine the number of households to whom you will need to send invitations. In general you will not need to send a separate invitation to every person on the list. (For more tips on wedding invitation etiquette, consult the FAQ section of the Appendix.)
- Determine the number of extra invitations you would like to order as mementos, for guests on your "B" list, or for any last-minute guests you may discover you forgot to invite.
- Determine the number of extra envelopes you will need to order. Keep in mind that you will make mistakes while addressing the invitations. A good rule of thumb would be to order approximately ten extra envelopes for every hundred invitations.

Now that you have determined what your stationery needs are, the least time-consuming and often least expensive route to purchasing your wedding invitations would be to order them from a catalog. Ordering from a catalog will not only save money but time, because it allows you and your fiancé to shop whenever and wherever it is convenient for you—over dinner, during your lunch break at work—you name it!

Consult advertisements in major bridal magazines for instructions on how to order copies of the invitation catalogs. Once the catalogs arrive and you have had the time to browse through them, call and request samples of any invitations in which you are particularly interested. Most companies will send you at least a few samples free of charge. Be sure to take advantage of this service and don't order any invitations without actually seeing and touching them first. It is sometimes difficult to judge the quality of paper and print on an invitation from catalog photographs.

If you choose to order from a local printer or stationer, you are usually restricted to viewing the sample books at their facility, as well as having to place your order and conduct all business at their store during business hours. However, the sample books at the printer and stationery shops typically contain real wedding invitations that you can immediately touch and feel to determine the quality of paper and printing styles.

If money is no object, there are many custom invitation specialists that can design creations using exquisite and unusual papers, fabrics, and accessories. A few of the finer stationery stores may carry a sample book of custom designs. You may also find some of these more elaborate invitations on display at a local bridal show. For additional leads, consult local telephone directories or regional bridal magazines.

Some additional invitation ordering tips include:

- If you are planning on addressing the invitations using a computer, do not pick an invitation with envelopes made out of extra thick paper (i.e., handmade or recycled paper). Thick envelopes will jam the printer and cause you much grief during the process.
- If you want to save money on postage, be sure that the invitations you order are not oversized and do not require additional postage. Your printer should be able to tell you this information, and many stationers indicate which items are oversized in their catalogs.
- To save money on stamps for the response card envelopes, consider using response postcards. Many stationers can print the same information onto a postcard format, which requires less postage.
- If you need to get all of your responses back in a hurry, sign up for a toll-free RSVP line. Consult bridal magazines or the Internet for leads on these services. Have the request for a response, a "respond by" date, and the phone number printed at the bottom of the invitation, or printed on a separate card. You may or may not save money using one of these services, but it could expedite the process. To definitely save money, use your home phone number as the response line. Be advised that etiquette watchdogs may frown on this more casual response method, as a written response to a wedding invitation is considered the most proper.

Finally, if you are considering sending wedding announcements after the wedding, please refer to Chapter Ten (see page 235).

HIRE A FLORIST

(Saturday Morning and/or Afternoon)

A good florist can have a great impact on your wedding's style—possibly more so than any other vendor you hire for the big day. But how do you find the perfect person to make your floral dreams a reality? As you may have already guessed, referrals from family, friends, and especially from your wedding consultant or ceremony and reception site coordinators are key. These types of referrals will not only lead you to someone with excellent floral design talents, but to someone who is reliable and can get all of the flowers to the ceremony and reception site, in good shape, and on time!

If you are looking for more leads, check out a local bridal show. There, many florists set up booths to display their work, along with photographs of weddings they've recently done. If you already happen to be a satisfied customer of a particular florist shop (and they're located close enough to your ceremony and reception site), ask them if they have experience servicing weddings as well. Though you may already be familiar with their work as a regular customer, be sure to request the names of, and speak to, at least one couple on whose wedding they've recently worked.

A comprehensive list of flowers that you may need to purchase for your wedding is included in the Florist Checklist (see page 124), but generally, couples rely on a professional florist to provide the following services:

- Floral bouquets for the bride and her attendants
- Boutonnieres for the groom, his attendants, the fathers of the bride and groom, the grandfathers of the bride and groom, and any other special relatives or friends
- Corsages for the mothers of the bride and groom, the grandmothers of the bride and groom, and any other special relatives or friends
- Appropriate flowers for any children in the wedding party, such as flower girls or ring bearers
- Floral decorations for the ceremony site
- Floral decorations and table centerpieces for the reception site

Once you have some prospective florists in mind, make appointments to meet with them. Before your appointment, do your homework and collect photographs of bouquets, boutonnieres, centerpieces, and other floral decorations that interest you, and then file them in your Portable Planner. Bring the planner containing your pictures and ideas to the appointment, to ensure that you can effectively communicate the floral look you want to achieve at your wedding.

If you don't find any photographs that sufficiently describe the flowers you are dreaming of, or if you are just unfamiliar with flowers in general, don't fret! Most reputable florists are equipped to show you photographs of different styles of bouquets and centerpieces, as well as examples of the individual flowers that comprise these arrangements. Most florists will also be able to recommend what flowers best suit your particular ceremony and reception site, the season, color scheme, and theme of your wedding, as well as your budget.

During your meeting with a florist, be sure that she takes detailed notes on the number, type, style, size, and color of the flowers you choose. Be sure that this information is included in a written price quote from the florist, and eventually is included in a written contract. Remember, as with most wedding vendors, florists will not reserve your wedding date on their calendar unless you have signed a contract and given them a deposit.

Finally, if you are considering having your bridal bouquet preserved after the wedding, please refer to Chapter Ten (see page 237).

HIRE A BAKER

(Saturday Morning and/or Afternoon)

Selecting a baker to create the perfect wedding cake should be one of the yummiest experiences you'll have during your wedding planning journey. It may surprise you how many of your friends and family will want to come along with you on this particular excursion. After all, what could be more fun than spending the weekend eating lots of cake?

To get started, ask all of your recently married friends and family for referrals to a good bakery. At first you may think that referrals are not essential to finding a good baker for your wedding cake. After all, if the cakes look and taste good, how can you go wrong? Where referrals can help is in assuring you that your baker has a solid track record of getting the cakes to the wedding reception on time, and in perfect shape. A lot can happen to a wedding cake in transit, but a good baker is experienced at handling these situations, and will not leave the wedding site until you have a perfectly displayed cake.

If you already frequent a particular bakery whose sweets you love, give it a call and ask if it has experience doing wedding cakes. Many bakers also display their work at local bridal shows, and bring along with them a variety of samples for you to try right on the spot.

When your research is done, make an appointment with the prospective baker. Usually wedding cake bakers will allow you to sample their different cake flavors during your appointment. Be sure to let them know in advance if there are any flavors that you are particularly interested in trying that day.

Before your appointment, don't forget to do your homework. Collect photos of wedding cake designs that interest you, and file them in your Portable Planner to take along. Most skilled bakers can re-create any cake design if they have a proper photograph of it. If, however, you are not already set on one particular design, the bakery will usually have plenty of display cakes to view, as well as numerous photos of cakes in their sample books.

When it comes time to order your wedding cake, you and your fiancé will not only have to decide on what style of cake to select, but also the cake's flavor, filling, icing type, and size (which may be a little tentative until you receive your final guest count for the reception). If you would like to freeze the top layer of your wedding cake to eat on your first anniversary, be sure to take that into account when determining the size of cake needed to feed all of your guests.

Also, don't forget to consider that many cake designs can be created from other types of desserts such as cheesecakes, or even ice cream. While these varieties will need to stay refrigerated longer, and will not be able to be displayed for as long a time as the standard baked cake, they will be a refreshing surprise for your guests and add a unique touch to your wedding reception.

When discussing your selections with the bakery, let it know if you are planning to decorate the cake with any additional accessories such as your own wedding cake topper, or fresh flowers. Ask if you can take a picture of the cake you have selected (if one is on display at the shop), or ask to make a color photocopy of the cake you selected out of their sample book. This will be a helpful tool for your florist, wedding consultant, caterer, or any other person to whom you delegate the responsibility of decorating the cake table.

Remember, as with all of your wedding vendors, you should get a written contract that includes all of the important details about the cake you ordered, as well as stating the location, date, and time the cake will be delivered. You will also need to give the bakery a deposit. Closer to your wedding date, if your guest count increases or decreases, be sure to let the bakery know so that they can adjust the size of the cake accordingly.

HIRE THE
MUSICAL ENTERTAINMENT

(Saturday Afternoon and/or Sunday)

With all the time, energy, and money you've already invested in creating the perfect environment for your wedding day, you can't forget that when the day finally rolls around, you want all of your guests to have a fun time as well. Hiring quality musical entertainment in the form of either live musicians or a disc jockey (DJ) will ensure that everyone will enjoy themselves during the wedding ceremony, and especially throughout the reception.

The site where you are holding your wedding ceremony will determine what type of musical entertainment you will need to hire. Many churches have a select group of musicians (i.e., an organist, soloist, guitarist, flutist, etc.) available for hire, or included with the use of the facility. At other venues it is up to you to decide what type of musicians (if any), you want, and can afford to hire for your ceremony.

When looking for talented ceremony musicians, whether they are guitarists, harpists, violinists, flutists, or vocalists, gather referrals and call around. Ask all potential musicians under consideration to send you a copy of their demo tape either on an audiocassette or, preferably, on videotape. If they do not have a demo tape available, ask to attend one of their upcoming performances to assess their talent and showmanship.

Also consult regional bridal magazines, the chamber of commerce, or your local telephone directory for listings of any entertainment consulting services. These companies represent a number of musicians and disc jockeys, and will usually have a whole library of demo tapes for you to listen to or view. To save some money, you may also consider hiring a music major from a local college to perform, or enlist the services of any talented musicians in the family, or your circle of friends.

If you don't find any musicians that you like or can afford, or if you decide you would rather not have live musicians performing at the ceremony, a disc jockey can be hired to play prerecorded music during appropriate parts of the ceremony. If you want to do this, be sure to approve the arrangement in advance with your site coordinator (especially if you are marrying in a place of worship). An economical option available at some ceremony locations is to use the venue's in-house audio system to play your own CDs or audiocassettes.

Whether you end up hiring a musician or a disc jockey, be sure to find out ahead of time if he is able to accommodate any special music requests you may have, and if so, how soon before the wedding you will need to turn in those requests. If you are having a cocktail hour after the ceremony, you may consider hiring the musicians to entertain your guests during this time as well.

Finding musical entertainment for your reception is a similar process to finding musical entertainment for your ceremony. Gather referrals for disc jockeys or bands from any friends or relatives, and then call these prospective entertainers to request a copy of their demo tape, as well as a song list.

When reviewing the work of a DJ or bandleader, determine if he is charismatic enough to lead your guests through all of the different events that will take place during your wedding reception. Also, determine how good of a job he will do at making your guests feel comfortable, and encouraging them to get out on the dance floor to have a good time. Review his song lists to get a better idea of what his music library or repertoire includes. Keep in mind that a good disc jockey or band should be able and willing to play the type of music that you and your fiancé decide is most appropriate for the occasion.

When you are ready to hire your musical entertainment, set up a meeting with the DJ and/or musicians to discuss your special needs. Be sure to get a written contract that includes the date, location, and time of your ceremony or reception. Also make sure it includes how many hours they are contracted to perform, what time they will be set up by, any equipment such as microphones, speakers, amplifiers, lights, or fog machines that are included in the price or will be brought along for an additional rental fee. Additionally, when hiring musicians, include their names and the type of instrument they play. If you are dealing with a company that represents many different disc jockeys, musicians, or bands, be sure that your contract clearly states the names of the entertainers you have selected.

A few weeks before the wedding don't forget to follow up with your disc jockey, musicians, or bandleader to confirm any special song requests or announcements that will need to be made during the reception or ceremony.

HIRE AN OFFICIANT

(Saturday Afternoon and/or Sunday) (Optional)

If you are getting married in a church, synagogue, or other venue where it is not necessary for you to hire your own officiant, you can skip this section altogether.

However, ceremony sites other than churches or synagogues provide only the use of their venue, and leave it up to the couple to hire their own officiant to perform the wedding service. If you are planning on having a civil ceremony, you will probably rely on the services of a judge, justice of the peace, or non-denominational minister to officiate. For religious ceremonies, you will need to find an officiant who is willing to perform the wedding service outside of his own place of worship.

To find an officiant, get referrals from your wedding consultant, family, friends, and your ceremony site coordinator. Also, consult regional bridal magazine advertisements or attend a local bridal show to find potential officiants. The only way you are really going to know if an officiant is "the right one" for your wedding is by meeting with him.

After you've done your research, set up an appointment for you and your fiancé to meet with the prospective officiants, and discuss what you are looking for in a wedding ceremony. The officiant should have some sample wedding services that he has written, and may even have a videotape of a recent service he has performed. If he is a practicing member of the clergy, you may also want to attend one of his upcoming services to get a better idea of his officiating style.

Once you have decided on the right officiant, be sure to discuss in advance whether or not you and your fiancé can add any personal touches to the wedding service, such as writing your own vows or having any special readings or musical solos performed. Also be sure to discuss whether a pre-marital counseling session is required or recommended, as well as if he is available and willing to conduct your wedding rehearsal. Lastly, get a written contract with your officiant that includes the agreed upon fee, the date, location, time, and length of your wedding ceremony.

THE WEDDING INVITATION CHECKLIST

(THIS IS A GUIDE FOR PRINTED ITEMS YOU MAY NEED TO CONSIDER.)

Item	Quantity	Cost Each
INVITATION ENSEMBLE		
☐ Inner Envelope	_____	_____
☐ Invitation	_____	_____
☐ Lined Outer Envelope	_____	_____
☐ Reception Card	_____	_____
☐ Reply Card	_____	_____
☐ Reply Envelope	_____	_____
ADDITIONAL ITEMS FOR INVITATION ENSEMBLE		
☐ Accommodation Cards	_____	_____
☐ Direction/Map Card	_____	_____
☐ Pew Card	_____	_____
ADDITIONAL ITEMS		
☐ At-Home Cards	_____	_____
☐ Engagement Announcements and Envelopes	_____	_____
☐ Escort Cards	_____	_____
☐ Informal Cards and Envelopes	_____	_____
☐ (Personalized) Matchbook Covers	_____	_____
☐ Menu Cards	_____	_____
☐ Name Cards	_____	_____

THE WEDDING INVITATION CHECKLIST (CONT'D)

☐ (Printed) Napkins   _____   _____

☐ Place Cards   _____   _____

☐ Thank-You Cards and Envelopes   _____   _____

☐ Wedding Announcements and Envelopes   _____   _____

☐ Wedding Programs   _____   _____

THE STATIONER

Name of Company: _____

Contact's Name: _____

Phone: _____ Fax: _____

E-mail: _____

Address: _____

QUESTIONS TO ASK

- When will you guarantee our invitation order will be ready?

- How will I receive them? (Will you ship them to my home or office? Do I have to pick them up from your store?)

- When will I be able to proofread the invitation text?

- What if I get the invitations back and there is a mistake:

    If it is an error on your company's part, will you reprint them at no cost to me? If so, how quickly?

    If we discover an error on our part, at what cost can we have the invitations reprinted? How long will it take?

- If we need additional invitations at a later date, at what cost can more copies be printed? Is there a minimum order amount for reprints? How quickly can reprints be made?

- Are any extra envelopes included in the cost of our order? At what cost can I order additional envelopes?

- When is the full payment due for our order? Do you require a deposit?

ADDITIONAL COMMENTS:

_____

_____

_____

_____

_____

_____

_____

THE FLORIST

Name of Company: _____

Contact's Name: _____

Phone: _____ Fax: _____

E-mail: _____

Address: _____

THE FLORIST CHECKLIST

(THIS IS A GUIDE FOR FLORAL ARRANGEMENTS
YOU MAY NEED TO CONSIDER.)

Item	Quantity	Cost Each
PERSONAL FLOWERS		
☐ Bride's Bouquet	_____	_____
☐ Bouquets—Maid/Matron of Honor	_____	_____
☐ Bridesmaids	_____	_____
☐ Groom's Boutonniere	_____	_____
☐ Boutonnieres—Best Man/Men		
Groomsmen/Ushers	_____	_____
☐ Flower Girls	_____	_____
☐ Junior Bridesmaids	_____	_____
☐ Ring Bearer	_____	_____
☐ Junior Groomsmen	_____	_____
☐ Mother of the Bride	_____	_____
☐ Mother of the Groom	_____	_____
☐ Grandmothers	_____	_____
☐ Grandfathers	_____	_____
☐ Godparents/Special Relatives	_____	_____
☐ Guest Book Attendant/Greeters	_____	_____
CEREMONY		
☐ Altar Arrangements	_____	_____
☐ Gazebo/Arch/Chuppah	_____	_____
☐ Pew/Aisle Decor	_____	_____

RECEPTION

- ☐ Cake Knife and Server
- ☐ Cake Table
- ☐ Fresh Flowers on Cake
- ☐ Guest Book Table
- ☐ Head Table
- ☐ Place Card Table
- ☐ Table Centerpieces
- ☐ Toasting Goblets
- ☐ Toss Bouquet
- ☐ Miscellaneous Decor:

QUESTIONS TO ASK

- What type of flowers will be in season around our wedding date?

- What suggestions do you have for the bridal bouquet? Can you explain the different styles?

- What suggestions do you have for flowers for the rest of the wedding party? Can you explain the different styles of bouquets, corsages, and boutonnieres?

- Can you provide us with samples?

- When is payment due in full for our order? Do you require a deposit?

- What is your cancellation policy?

- What type of guarantee do you offer on the freshness and quality of your flowers?

THE FLORIST CHECKLIST (CONT'D)

- What is your policy on substituting the flowers that I have selected? (What happens if the flowers I select are not available on the wedding day?)

- What time will you arrive to deliver flowers to the ceremony site? By what time will all of the flowers be completely set up at the ceremony site?

- What time will you deliver the flowers to the reception site? By what time will all of the flowers be completely set up at the reception site?

- Will you decorate our wedding cake with flowers if we choose to do so?

- Are there any additional costs for delivery, travel, or set-up time? Is there an additional fee for setting up at two locations (the ceremony site and the reception site)?

- Will you be the contact person on site the day of the wedding? If not, who will it be? At what phone number (or pager, or cellular phone number) can I best reach someone that day if there are any problems?

- Can you provide other accessories such as an aisle runner, columns, candelabras, or potted plants? At what cost? Is there a security deposit required?

- If I need to add to my floral order (i.e., additional centerpieces, bouquets, boutonnieres), what is the deadline for changes?

- Are you familiar with the ceremony site? If yes, how would you recommend we decorate it? If no, will you be willing to visit the site with me?

- Are you familiar with the reception site? If yes, how would you recommend we decorate it? If no, will you be willing to visit the site with me?

- Will you need a map or driving instructions to any of the locations?

- Will you need any special equipment, such as a ladder, at the ceremony site? At the reception site?

- Will you preserve my bouquet after the wedding? If no, can you recommend a company that will?

ADDITIONAL COMMENTS:

_____

_____

_____

_____

_____

_____

THE BAKER

Name of Company: _____

Contact's Name: _____

Phone: _____ Fax: _____

E-mail: _____

Address: _____

Dates Available: _____

QUESTIONS TO ASK

- Are there any specialty cakes for which your bakery is known?

THE BAKER (cont'd)

- What are your most popular wedding cake flavors and styles?

- Can we choose different cake flavors for different tiers?

- Which wedding cake flavors freeze the best (if we want to freeze our top layer to eat on our first anniversary)?

- Do you provide a cake box in which to store the top layer?

- What is the deadline for making any changes to the cake flavors or style?

- Can you create a cake design if I provide you with a photograph as a reference?

- When our final guest count is in, can we increase or decrease the size of our cake?

- When is the deadline to make any of those changes?

- When is the full payment due for our order? Do you require a deposit?

- Does the cost include delivery and set-up time?

- How is the cake transported to the reception site?

- Will you guarantee that the cake will arrive in good shape and be properly displayed at our reception?

- What time will you deliver the wedding cake?

- Will you be the contact person on site the day of my wedding? If not, who will it be? At what phone number (or pager, or cellular phone number) can I best reach someone that day if there are any problems?

- Are you familiar with the reception site? Will you need a map or driving instructions?

ADDITIONAL COMMENTS:

_____

_____

_____

_____

THE MUSICAL ENTERTAINMENT

Name of Company: _____

Contact's Name: _____

Musician/Disc Jockey's Name (if different from above): ____

Phone: _____ Fax: _____

E-mail: _____

Address: _____

Dates Available: _____

QUESTIONS TO ASK

- How would you describe your musical style (for ceremony musicians or band)?

- How would you describe your music library (for disc jockey)?

- Will you need any special equipment (chairs, music stands, microphones, access to electrical outlets, speakers, amplifiers, etc.) on site at the ceremony or reception?

- Will you be able to get any songs that we request? When would we have to turn in any special requests to you (for disc jockey)?

- If any of our requests are new songs, how much time will you need to learn the music (for band)?

THE MUSICAL ENTERTAINMENT
(CONT'D)

- Will you take requests from our guests on our wedding day?

- Will you also serve as emcee during our wedding? When do we have to give you any information regarding announcements?

- How will you (and your band members) be dressed on our wedding day?

- When is payment due in full? Do you require a deposit?

- Do you charge a flat rate or an hourly rate?

- If we need you to stay longer than planned on our wedding day, are you open to that? At what rate do you charge for additional time?

- Is travel time included in your rate?

- Is set-up time included in your rate?

- How many breaks will you need to take in between sets? How long will the breaks be? Will you play prerecorded music during these breaks (for bands)?

- Are you familiar with the ceremony site?

- Are you familiar with the reception site?

- Will you need a map or driving instructions?

ADDITIONAL COMMENTS:

_____

_____

_____

_____

_____

_____

THE OFFICIANT

Name of Church/Company: _____

Contact's Name: _____

Officiant's Name (if different from above): _____

Phone: _____   Fax: _____

E-mail: _____

Address: _____

Dates Available: _____

QUESTIONS TO ASK

- Describe the type of wedding services you usually perform. Do you have any samples of text?

- Typically, how long are the services you perform? Can we request a longer or a shorter service?

- May we write our own vows?

- Can we personalize our wedding service in any way? May we have special readings or a song performed during the ceremony?

- Is premarital counseling required or recommended?

- Will you need a microphone for the ceremony?

- Will you need a lectern or any other special equipment?

- What attire do you wear during the service?

- Are you available to conduct our wedding rehearsal?

- Are you familiar with the ceremony site?

- Will you need a map or driving instructions?

- When is the full payment due for your services? Do you require a deposit?

ADDITIONAL COMMENTS:

_____

_____

_____

_____

_____

_____

_____

_____

_____

_____

_____

_____

_____

_____

_____

_____

_____

_____

_____

_____

_____

_____

_____

Weekend Four Checklist

☐ Set Up the Bridal Gift Registry

☐ Make the Honeymoon Plans

☐ Secure Accommodations for the

 Out-of-Town Guests

☐ Shop for the Wedding Rings

☐ Finalize the Guest List

☐ Collect the Addresses of the Invited Guests

SET UP THE
BRIDAL GIFT REGISTRY

(Friday Evening and/or Saturday)

Setting up a bridal gift registry at a department store or specialty store provides a convenient way for your guests to know what you and your fiancé need and want as gifts for your wedding. Though it may seem a little presumptuous at first—picking out your own wedding gifts—most of your guests will appreciate and often count on having the guidance of a registry when shopping for the wedding, as well as any shower gifts.

Going into the registry process prepared will save you and your fiancé a lot of grief. Picking selections for the gift registry may seem like an easy and fun process that doesn't require a whole lot of preplanning. However, what most couples don't realize is that unless some ground rules are set, you may find yourselves bickering in the aisles of the department store over something as trivial as whether or not you really need a Belgian waffle maker.

Before registering anywhere, sit down with your fiancé and discuss the following topics about the home you will share as husband and wife:

How will we decorate our bedroom and bathrooms?
- In what color and/or theme will we decorate our bedroom?
- What size sheets will we need for our bed? How many sets? What type of comforter and blankets?
- In what color and/or theme will we decorate our bathroom?
- How many towels would we like? How many of each size?

How will we outfit and decorate our kitchen and dining room?
- In what color and/or theme will we decorate our kitchen?
- In what color and/or theme will we decorate our dining room?
- What type of table linens will we need? What size tablecloth? How many napkins? How many place mats?
- Will we want fine china? If so, how many place settings?
- Will we want any plates for casual dining? If so, how many place settings?

- Will we want flatware? Formal, casual, or both? How many place settings of each?
- Will we want glassware? Formal, casual, or both? How many of each?
- Will we want any pots or pans?
- Will we want any small appliances?
- Will we want any cutlery?

How much entertaining do we think we will be doing?

How much storage space will we have in our home?

Is there anything other than housewares for which we need or want to register?

The decisions that you make about what you need and want for your home will help you to determine the most appropriate store at which to register, but when selecting a store, do more than just review the merchandise it carries. Consider the quality of customer service it can offer you and your fiancé as the registrants, as well as how well it will service your family and friends while they are shopping for you.

Also, research if the store has an equitable return policy. This is important because despite your guests' best efforts, you will often receive duplicate wedding gifts that will need to be exchanged or returned after the wedding. Ask about any discounts that the store may offer to registered couples who want to purchase the remaining items after the wedding, to complete their registry. This type of discount can be extremely beneficial if, for example, you only receive two of the twelve flatware place settings you registered for, and want to purchase the remaining ten to complete the set. If many of your guests reside out of town, find out if your registry will be available via a nationwide network, or if your guests can shop over the phone, through catalogs, by fax, or over the Internet.

Before registering at any store, call ahead and find out if an appointment is necessary. When making selections, choose gifts from all different price ranges. Also be sure to include enough items appropriate for shower or other prewedding party gifts.

If none of the registries available at local department stores or specialty shops suit you and your fiancé's interests, you may want to consider setting up a less traditional type of registry. Other options include registering at a home improvement store, a sporting goods store, a travel agency, or even a charitable organization that will accept donations from your guests in lieu of gifts.

Doing a search on the Internet using the keywords "bridal registry," "gift registry," or "wedding registry" will uncover many other nontraditional outlets offering gift registries. What these companies can offer, which most department stores cannot, is the opportunity to create a registry from a wide variety of gifts. Most will also let you and your fiancé make your registry selections on-line, and will allow your guests to shop via catalogs, over the phone, or directly over the Internet.

MAKE THE HONEYMOON PLANS

(Saturday Morning)

There is no better way to kick off your new status as husband and wife than by taking a well-deserved romantic getaway after your wedding celebration. Before you can start packing your suitcases, however, you and your fiancé will have to decide on what type of trip you want to take, how much money you can afford to spend on it, and how much time you can take off from work or other commitments. Unless you want your honeymoon destination to be a surprise, exchange ideas with your fiancé about any destinations you have always wanted to visit, and the types of activities you want to have available during your trip.

The most popular types of honeymoon trips that couples consider include:

- **The Resort Getaway:** This could include a trip to a tropical island resort, a golf or spa resort, or a mountain/ski resort.
- **The City Getaway:** This could include a trip to a city nearby, or to a city on the other side of the world.
- **The Adventure Getaway:** This could include a backpacking trip, a trip to a tropical rain forest, a dude ranch excursion, or a safari.

- **An Ocean Cruise:** This could include a trip on a large cruise ship, or a chartered voyage on a smaller vessel such as a sailboat.

Once you have decided on the type of honeymoon trip you wish to take, research specific locations and accommodations that fit into this category. Consult a travel agent for brochures, search the Internet, and read up on these locations in bridal, honeymoon, and travel magazines. Don't forget to get referrals from any well-traveled friends or relatives, as well as from any newlyweds that you may know.

When you have narrowed down your choices to one or two specific destinations, do some additional homework before booking the trip. Find out what the expected weather conditions will be during the time of year you will be traveling. Also find out if any large festivals or conventions are planned for the time of year you will be visiting. Depending on what the planned events are, these activities may be an extra added bonus, or a deterrent for wanting to be there during your honeymoon. If you are traveling internationally, check out the current exchange rates, as well as what type of documentation or immunizations you will need to travel into that country.

When you are ready to book your trip, it's advisable to use the services of a professional travel agent with expertise in honeymoon and/or resort bookings. Be sure to ask her:

- To verify what type of documents or immunizations are necessary to travel to your honeymoon destination
- To issue any tickets or reservations for the bride under her maiden name (or whatever name appears on her identification). It is extremely important to have the names on your travel documents match the names on your identification—especially if you are traveling internationally.
- To request any special meals when making airline reservations

Your honeymoon vacation will likely be the most romantic, as well as most expensive, vacation you will ever take. You don't want to take any chances! So protect your investment and ask your travel agent what type of travel insurance policy you can purchase. Though it may seem like an unnecessary expense, the cost of the policy will be insignificant compared to the price of making any last-minute travel changes should weather, or political conditions, bar you from traveling according to your original itinerary.

Once you have booked your trip, you should immediately start taking care of some of the following tasks:

- Apply for or renew your passport (if you don't already have a valid one, be sure to apply for it under your maiden name or the name that appears on your other forms of valid identification).
- Apply for any visas that are required.
- Consult your physician for advice on when you should come in to receive mandatory or recommended immunizations.
- If you are traveling to a country where they speak another language, you may want to enroll in a basic language course, or purchase a book or cassette tape that can teach you what you need to know to get around.
- For those couples with pets, make any kennel reservations or find a pet-sitter as soon as possible.
- For those couples with homes that require substantial maintenance, find a house-sitter as soon as possible.

Throughout your vacation planning, make sure that everyone from the airline, to the hotel, to the rental car company knows that you are honeymooners. You will be surprised by all the perks and special attention that comes along with being newlyweds!

SECURE ACCOMMODATIONS FOR THE OUT-OF-TOWN GUESTS

(Saturday Morning)

If any of your guests will be traveling to your wedding from out of town, they will certainly appreciate any advice you can offer them regarding accommodations. Most hotels, motels, and inns will allow you to reserve a block of rooms for your guests, and may offer a discounted group rate.

When you are ready to reserve a block of rooms, you will need to speak to someone in reservations, or the hotel representative that handles group sales. There are usually a minimum number of rooms that you will need to reserve in order to qualify for a discounted group rate. After making arrangements with the hotel or inn, be sure that it sends you a written confirmation that includes the number of rooms reserved, the rates, and the dates they are reserved for.

When all of the arrangements are made, you can begin spreading the word to your family and friends about the reservations you have made. Be sure to ask the hotel or inn what the best phone number (preferably toll free) is for your guests to call and make their reservations. Make sure that your guests know to identify themselves with your wedding group. Many hotels will even provide you with printed cards with all of the necessary information that you can distribute to your guests, or enclose with the wedding invitations.

SHOP FOR THE
WEDDING RINGS

(Saturday Afternoon and/or Sunday)

The wedding rings you exchange will be an everlasting reminder of the vows you make to one another. For this reason, finding the perfect rings to express your union is a very important detail for most couples. Fortunately, most jewelry stores carry a wide variety of wedding rings from which couples can choose.

Before heading out on your shopping trip, discuss the budget for each ring with your fiancé, as well as the style of ring you would each like to have. Some specific questions to ask each other would include:

- Do we want matching or nonmatching rings?
- Of what type metal do we want our rings to be made (gold, white gold, platinum, silver)?
- Do we want plain metal bands or bands adorned with jewels?
- Will we want to put engraved inscriptions inside our rings? If yes, what will they read?
- What style ring works best with the bride's engagement ring (if she plans on wearing them both together)?

When trying on rings at the jewelry store, consider not only the way the ring looks on your finger, but also how comfortable it is to wear. You will be wearing these rings every day for the rest of your life so be sure that they feel comfortable.

Most couples find it helpful to use the same jeweler from whom they purchased the engagement ring. Assuming the jeweler did a good job the first time around, you will have the assurance of knowing that she can provide a certain quality of product and service. Whichever jeweler you decide to use, be sure to allow enough time for your wedding rings to be made or ordered. Don't forget to allow enough time between the delivery of the rings and the wedding date, in case any re-sizing or engraving needs to be done.

FINALIZE
THE GUEST LIST

(Sunday Afternoon)

Now that the majority of the decision making for your wedding planning is done, you should have enough information to finalize the names on the wedding guest list. Sit down with your fiancé (and your respective families if you choose), and review the preliminary guest list that was created during Weekend One. Look it over to make sure that there are no special people in your lives that were unintentionally left off the list. If you divided your list into "A" and "B" categories, decide which "A's" are still "A's," and if there is room for any "B's" to be added.

As you work on revising the list, keep in mind how many guests your wedding and reception site can comfortably accommodate, as well as how many guests your budget can bear. If your planning has left you on, or below budget, you may not have to change much at all. However, if you are over budget, one of the most effective (but certainly not the most painless) ways to get back on track is to reduce the number of guests on the guest list. Reducing the guest list will not only save you money in your reception catering budget, but can also reduce the amount of money you will have to spend on the rental of chairs, plates, silverware, and glassware, as well as parking fees, table centerpieces, and wedding favors.

COLLECT THE ADDRESSES
OF THE INVITED GUESTS

(Sunday Evening)

The ease of this next wedding task completely depends on how up-to-date your address book is.

Collecting the current addresses of all of your invited guests can be either a simple step or a fairly time-consuming one. But if you employ the help of your fiancé, your family, and friends, it can all be accomplished during the course of one evening.

If you have a lot of missing addresses, first consult the address books of your family members and close friends to fill in the blanks. Then call, fax, or E-mail only those guests whose information is still lacking. If you do not have the time to make all of these queries yourself, get the help of a willing family member or friend, and have this person make some of the requests for you.

While you are gathering the addresses, there are several ways to keep it all organized. Create an alphabetized handwritten or computer-generated list that includes your guests' names and addresses. Leave enough space by each entry to place a check mark after the invitation has been sent, and a check mark after a thank-you note has been sent. Include room to write down their responses, and any gifts given. Instead of creating a list, the same information can also be entered into an inexpensive address book purchased expressly for this purpose, or each guest's information can be printed onto an index card that can be filed alphabetically in a box. If you are using wedding planning software, the guest list format is often already set up for you.

Make sure that all of the addresses on your guest list are correct. You don't want to risk your guests' invitations being delayed in the mail, or have to go through the hassle or expense of remailing invitations that get returned due to incorrect addressing. All of your planning will make the invitation addressing tasks that you will accomplish during Weekend Five move along much more smoothly.

THE BRIDAL GIFT REGISTRY

Name of Store/Company:

Contact's Name:

Phone: Fax:

E-mail:

Address:

Date of Appointment:

QUESTIONS TO ASK

- What is your store's return policy?

- Is there nationwide access to the registry? What access is available from out of the country?

- Can my guests shop from our registry over the phone? By fax? Over the Internet? By using catalogs?

- Will you ship gifts to our home? At what cost? What type of shipping? Is a signature required for delivery?

- Do you offer any discounts to registered couples who want to purchase additional items after the wedding, to complete the registry?

- Do you give out bridal registry cards that we can include in any shower invitations?

- How long will our registry stay in your system?

- How soon after guests make purchases is the registry updated?

- Can we continue to add/delete selections to our registry after the initial appointment? How soon after will these changes be reflected on the registry?

- Do you normally keep our china pattern in stock? Our flatware in stock? Our fine crystal?

- From what departments can I make registry selections?

- Do you issue gift receipts when my guests purchase from the registry?

- Do you offer complimentary gift-wrapping?

ADDITIONAL COMMENTS:

_____

_____

_____

_____

THE HONEYMOON

Name of Travel Agency/Company: _____

Contact's Name: _____

Phone: _____ Fax: _____

E-mail: _____

Address: _____

Dates Available: _____

QUESTIONS TO ASK

- What type of travel do you specialize in?

- Will we be traveling to our destination during the high or low season?

THE HONEYMOON (CONT'D)

- What are the advantages and disadvantages of traveling during this time?

- What type of weather is typical for that time of year?

- Does the establishment offer any special perks or discounts for honeymooners?

- How popular is this destination with honeymooners? Why or why not?

- Will there be any special festivals, conventions, or anything else going on during the time of year we will be traveling that we should know about?

- When is payment due in full for our trip? Is a deposit required? How much and when is it due?

- What is the cancellation policy?

- What type of travel insurance is available? What specifically does it cover?

- What types of upgrades are available at this location? On this airline?

- Can I use any frequent flier miles toward this flight, hotel room, or rental car?

- Will I need a passport?

- What type of currency do they accept? Do they accept most credit cards? Do they accept most ATM cards?

- How many honeymoons do you book a year?

- What has some of the feedback been from a few of your recent honeymooners?

- Have you personally visited this destination? What were your impressions? If not, what were some of the impressions from other couples you have sent there?

ADDITIONAL COMMENTS:

_____

_____

_____

THE GUEST ACCOMMODATIONS

Name of Facility: _____

Contact's Name: _____

Phone: _____ Fax: _____

E-mail: _____

Address: _____

Dates Available: _____

QUESTIONS TO ASK

- What is the minimum and maximum number of rooms I can reserve for my guests around the dates of our wedding?

- At what rate per night will you guarantee the rooms? At what rate for suites?

- What amenities does your facility have?

- What amenities do each of the guest rooms have?

- Do you have a honeymoon suite available if my fiancé and I choose to stay there as well?

THE GUEST ACCOMMODATIONS
(CONT'D)

- Will your staff be flexible about early check-in times/late checkout times for our guests?

- Will your staff be willing to deliver gift baskets to my guests' rooms, or hand them out as they check in?

- Does your hotel offer any shuttle services? Is this something your staff is willing to arrange?

ADDITIONAL COMMENTS:

_____

_____

_____

THE WEDDING RING JEWELER

Name of Store/Jeweler: _____

Contact's Name: _____

Phone: _____   Fax: _____

E-mail: _____

Address: _____

QUESTIONS TO ASK

- When will you guarantee that our wedding rings will be ready?

- When is payment due in full?

- Is a deposit required?

- Will you re-size the rings if necessary? Will there be an additional cost for this service? How long will it take?

- Can we put engraved inscriptions on these types of rings? How long can they be? At what cost will you do them, or is this service included in the price?

- If we choose to, can the bride's wedding ring be attached to her engagement ring? If yes, at what cost, or is this service included in the price?

ADDITIONAL COMMENTS:

_____

_____

_____

_____

_____

_____

_____

_____

_____

_____

_____

_____

_____

_____

_____

_____

_____

ADDITIONAL COMMENTS:

_____

_____

_____

_____

_____

_____

_____

_____

_____

_____

_____

_____

_____

_____

_____

_____

_____

_____

_____

_____

_____

_____

_____

Weekend Five Checklist

☐ Address the Invitations

☐ Meet with the Hair and Makeup Artist

☐ Meet with or Contact Other Vendors

☐ Develop the Ceremony Outline

☐ Develop the Reception Outline

ADDRESS THE INVITATIONS

(Friday Evening and/or Saturday Evening and/or Sunday Evening)

Addressing wedding invitations is potentially a tedious and time-consuming task for you and your fiancé—especially if you are having a large wedding. If you have the money in your budget, and want to save yourself valuable time, consider enlisting the services of a professional calligrapher. A calligrapher can beautifully address the invitations according to the guest list you provide her, and will usually charge a fee per envelope or per line. Most likely you will still have to assemble and stamp the invitations yourself, but you will definitely appreciate having one less step to accomplish.

If hiring a professional calligrapher is out of the question, consider asking a talented friend or family member for help with the calligraphy or printing. You may be surprised by how many people are willing to help out. If you have a substantial amount of invitations to address, you may want to throw an "invitation addressing party." Invite your family, some friends, or members of the wedding party over and make it a group effort. Even if some of your helpers do not have great penmanship, they will still be invaluable help assembling, stamping, and sealing the invitations.

If both you, and the people you know, lack the penmanship skills and the time to address the invitations by hand, consider addressing the envelopes using your home or work computer. With the right equipment it's fairly easy to print the addresses directly onto the envelopes, using a nice formal font. Though some etiquette watchdogs may frown on this method, using a computer will save you valuable time, and can create just as nice of an impression as hand printing.

If your guest list is not already entered into a computer database or a wedding planning program, it may take some time to input all of the pertinent information. In the future, however, you will have a useful document to track your guests' responses and any gifts they have given, as well as have the tools to automatically address any thank-you notes or additional wedding-related correspondence.

Keep in mind that if your wedding invitations are being engraved or created by any other specialized form of printing, they may not be completed by this weekend. You might have to postpone this particular weekend goal until a later date, when the invitations are done.

When you are ready to begin the addressing process, there are a few important steps you should take care of first:

1. **Check for Accuracy:** Check, double check, and triple check all of the information on your invitations for accuracy. Make sure that all of the names are spelled correctly. Be sure that the date, time, and location for the ceremony and the reception are accurate. Review any maps or directions to the site. Make sure that no highway or road construction along the route will cause any detours.

2. **Purchase the Necessary Postage:** Take one completely assembled invitation to the post office and weigh it to determine the proper amount of postage necessary. Keep in mind that if the invitation is made up of heavy paper stock, the envelope is oversized, or if multiple inserts have been included, additional postage is often required. As a courtesy to your guests, don't forget to purchase stamps for the response card envelopes as well. Most likely, the postage for the response cards will cost less than the postage for the invitations. Don't forget you can save yourself a lot of grief by purchasing self-adhesive stamps. Your tongue will thank you for it later!

3. **Review the Proper Etiquette:** Take the time before you start assembling and addressing your invitations to become familiar with the proper etiquette. Most printers will include information on wedding invitation etiquette with your order. You can also consult wedding invitation catalogs, bridal magazines, or the FAQ section of the Appendix for more tips on invitation etiquette.

4. **Develop a System:** Before you dive into the addressing process, set aside enough workspace in your home for an invitation assembly line. Then develop a system of how you are going to get it all done. One effective system includes performing the following steps:

   1. Address Outer Envelopes
   2. Address Inner Envelopes
   3. Stamp Response Card Envelopes
   4. Assemble Invitations
   5. Seal Envelopes (outer envelopes only)
   6. Stamp Outer Envelopes
   7. Check Off Names on Guest List as Invitations are Complete

8. Mail Invitations (These should be sent out four to six weeks before the wedding date. If any need to be mailed internationally, they should be sent about eight weeks in advance.)

MEET WITH
THE HAIR AND
MAKEUP ARTIST

(Saturday Morning)

Hiring a talented hair and makeup artist will ensure that you look and feel as beautiful as possible on your wedding day. When searching for the perfect wedding day beautician, many brides need not look any further than their own personal hair stylists. If you already have someone you entrust with your hair, ask her if she has experience styling and applying makeup for weddings. Keep in mind that styling hair and makeup for a wedding is much different from styling hair and makeup for everyday wear.

If you cannot use your own stylist, ask your wedding consultant or any recent brides or bridesmaids that you know for references. You can also consult advertisements in regional bridal magazines or the telephone directory. Another place to look is local bridal shows, where hair and makeup artists set up booths and offer free consultations and bridal makeovers on the spot.

As with all of your other wedding vendors, try to enlist the services of someone whose personality won't add any undue stress to you or your attendants on the wedding day. When you have found someone that you like and are interested in hiring, set up an appointment for a consultation. During the consultation, the hair and makeup artist will try different hairstyles on you, and will apply wedding day–style makeup as a "test run" for the big day.

When calling to set up your appointment time, inquire if she prefers or requires you to bring any of your own cosmetics such as eyeliner, mascara, an eyelash curler, or lipstick. Also find out if she wants you to, or doesn't want you to, wash your hair on the day of the consultation. Many stylists prefer that you have some built-up oils and dirt in the hair when creating upswept hairstyles, because they add texture, and help to hold the hairstyle in place.

On the day of your consultation be prepared to bring along the following items:

- Your headpiece and/or veil.
- Photos of any hair or makeup styles that you like.
- A photo of your wedding dress. It will also be helpful to bring along a photo of your bridesmaid dresses, as well as photos of your bridal bouquet if possible.
- A video camera and/or still camera to have someone take photographs of your finished hair and makeup from different angles and in different types of light (indoor and outdoor). This not only makes a great memento for your scrapbook but also lets you look at the hairstyle and makeup application later on to determine if you want to change or adjust anything for the wedding day. For the beautician, it serves as a reminder of the hairstyle you selected.
- White or off-white clothing (or whatever color your wedding dress is). Wear these colors to the appointment. You may also find it helpful to wear a blouse with a similar neckline as your wedding dress.

If you like the work the hair and makeup artist does during the consultation, make arrangements to have her provide the same service on your wedding day. Discuss whether she will do your hair and makeup at the ceremony site, at a nearby home or hotel room, or at her own salon. Also decide whether she will provide hair and makeup services for your attendants, your mother, and future mother-in-law, and at what cost. Before you leave, ask for any beauty maintenance tips regarding your hair, hair coloring, and skin.

After the consultation, try to keep your hair and makeup intact for as long as possible. Test it out to see how long it wears throughout the day. Keep in mind, you will be at your wedding for a long time—so it is important that your makeup application and hairstyle last for a long time too.

Even if you are not planning on hiring a professional to do your hair and makeup, it is still a good idea to use this time to do a test run yourself. After all, you don't want to risk having a bad hair day on your wedding day, do you?

MEET WITH OR
CONTACT OTHER VENDORS

(Saturday Afternoon)

By this point, you will have hired the majority of your wedding day vendors. However, you may want to take this opportunity to hire additional vendors to handle services such as: transportation to and from the ceremony and reception site (via limousine, town car, horse and carriage, etc.), valet parking, coat check and/or lounge attendants, child care, favor making, or any other special touches you would like included on your wedding day.

As with all of your other wedding vendors, it is important to start off your search by getting referrals from friends and family. Especially with the vendors handling your transportation and parking needs, you want to be sure that they are reliable, safe, and carry the proper amount of liability insurance.

When hiring a limousine or other means of transportation, discuss in advance what year, make, model, and color of vehicle they will guarantee for your wedding day. Know that some limousine companies, for example, will charge more for the rental of a white limousine than for any other color. Don't assume that you will have your pick of vehicles all for the same rate. When reserving a block of time for your transportation, allow enough time to account for any delays. Have an agreement with the transportation company in advance as to what rate you will be billed for any overtime that may be incurred.

When hiring valet parking attendants, be sure that they come highly recommended by the ceremony or reception site coordinator. Find out if they are familiar with the site's parking layout and restrictions, or if they have any problem adhering to the rules set forth by the site's management.

If you are expecting many guests with small children, or if any members of your immediate families or the wedding party will be bringing their babies or young children to the wedding, you may consider setting up child care during the ceremony. Ask an experienced baby-sitter to be on hand at the ceremony site a little before, and during, the ceremony to watch any children that may not be able to sit quietly through the entire service. You may want to consider making similar arrangements for the reception as well.

Discuss this option with your ceremony site coordinator to make sure that there is an appropriate area for the baby-sitter and children to remain during the wedding service. Once you have made these arrangements, you can begin to spread the word to those guests with children. Another alternative is to ask your groomsmen, ushers, wedding consultant, a friend, or a relative to greet any guests with children as they arrive at the ceremony site to inform them of the child care options you have arranged.

DEVELOP THE CEREMONY OUTLINE

(Sunday Afternoon)

About now, most of the pieces of your wedding planning puzzle should be falling nicely into place. The playing field is set, the team members have their uniforms, and now is the time to devise a basic game plan for the "big day." Developing a ceremony outline will ensure that your wedding service contains all of the important elements that you and your fiancé desire, and that it is executed in a flowing manner. Later on (about three weeks before the wedding date—see Chapter Six), you will use this information, or have your wedding consultant use this information, to complete the ceremony portion of the master wedding day itinerary.

If your officiant will be performing a strict religious ceremony, you may have little to no input on the structure and content of the marriage service. Your only means to personalize the service may come from being allowed to select certain readings, devising the order of the processional and recessional, or perhaps by choosing any of the musical pieces performed during the ceremony. Your officiant may, however, allow you to add a few ceremonial touches such as the lighting of a unity candle, or a floral presentation to the parents. These are all items you should have already discussed with your officiant during the initial meeting. If you have not already done so, be sure to bring these matters up with him during your next appointment (there is time allotted for this during Weekend Six).

If your officiant is willing to work with you and your fiancé to create a more personalized wedding service, try to familiarize yourself with the basic components that go into a traditional wedding. Once you have done so, and are familiar with the different parts of the ceremony and their meanings, you can begin to think of ways to specialize your own service. The following items traditionally make up the wedding ceremony:

The Prelude: This is anything that takes place before the actual start of the ceremony. Many couples arrange for musicians to play, or have a vocalist perform, a variety of songs as their guests find their seats. This may also be a time to prepare any special touches for the ceremony, such as having the ushers light candles.

The Processional: This is how the officiant, the family, the wedding party, and the bride and groom reach their respective places at the front of the ceremony site. Processionals vary from wedding to wedding for many reasons, including religious or ethnic traditions, the layout and space constraints of the ceremony site, the number of people in the wedding party, and the personal preferences of the bride and groom. A typical processional would be ordered as follows:

- The **Officiant** takes his place in front of the ceremony site.
- The **Groom** followed by the **Best Man** take their places in front of the ceremony site.
- The **Groom's Parents** are seated.
- The **Bride's Mother** is seated.
- The **Groomsmen** and the **Bridesmaids** walk down the aisle in pairs (usually in order of height, most often from shortest to tallest), and take their places in front of the ceremony site. The Bridesmaids can also walk down the aisle alone if you choose to have the Groomsmen take their places earlier, following the Groom and the Best Man.
- The **Maid/Matron of Honor** walks down the aisle. She can also be escorted by the Best Man if you choose not to have him enter earlier with The Groom.
- The **Ring Bearer** and **Flower Girl** walk down the aisle (one following the other, or paired together) preceding the Bride.
- The **Bride** is escorted down the aisle by the **Father of the Bride**.

With processionals, realize that many varieties exist! Do what works best for your particular situation. If you have any questions, look to your officiant, wedding consultant, or ceremony site coordinator for advice.

The Welcome or Greeting: These opening remarks by the officiant extend a welcome to all of your guests, and could include a few words about why everyone is "gathered here today." The officiant may also briefly explain the significance of certain parts of the wedding ceremony.

Opening Readings and/or Prayers: These opening words of inspiration can be read by the officiant, or by any readers that you and your fiancé select. The readings and prayers are selected by either the officiant or by the couple.

Musical Pieces and/or Solos: An instrumental or a vocal rendition of a song or hymn may be performed in honor of the couple. Most couples can select the music and the performers, though for some religious ceremonies the music must be "approved" and deemed appropriate for the occasion.

The Giving Away/ Recognition of the Parents: Traditionally, the bride is "given away" by her father when the officiant asks "Who gives this woman to be married to this man?" and he responds "I do." Nowadays, more couples are opting for the bride to be "given away" by both her mother and her father, by having her father respond "Her mother and I do," or having them both respond "We do." Another popular variation is to recognize both the bride's and the groom's parents by having the officiant ask "Who blesses" or "Who supports this marriage?" To this question, both sets of parents can respond in unison "We do."

The Charge to the Couple: This part of the ceremony signifies that each member of the couple voluntarily enters into the marriage. The officiant will ask the bride and groom separately, "Will you take this man/woman to be your husband/wife?"

The Exchange of Vows: The bride and groom will take turns reciting either traditional vows set forth by their religion, vows written by their officiant, or may even decide to write their own vows.

The Ring Ceremony: The bride and groom each take a turn slipping a wedding ring on the other's ring finger. While doing this they exchange pledges about what the ring symbolizes, and usually start off the pledges by saying "with this ring . . ."

Prayers for the Couple/Thoughts on Marriage: The officiant, or any special family members or friends (with your officiant's approval) may offer a special prayer for the couple, or share some special words on love and marriage.

The Charge to the Guests: The officiant will challenge the guests to support and pray for the marriage of the new couple.

Special Celebrations: These could include any ethnic or religious wedding traditions such as the lighting of a unity candle, or any other symbolic gesture that the couple would like to perform on the occasion of their marriage.

The Pronouncement: This is when the officiant announces that the couple is legally married. Most officiants include the words "I now pronounce you man and wife," or the more egalitarian "I now pronounce you husband and wife."

The Kiss: What more can we say about this one, other than it is technically the last part of the pronouncement. Oh yes—practice as much as you need to, to get it just right.

The Presentation: The officiant may end the service by presenting the newly married couple to their guests. He will usually include the words "I present to you for the first time Mr. and Mrs. . . ."

The Recessional: The order in which the bride and groom, the wedding party, family, and officiant depart the ceremony site immediately after the conclusion of the service. In most cases, the processional is organized as follows:

- **The Bride and Groom**
- **The Ring Bearer and Flower Girl** paired together.
- **The Maid/Matron of Honor and the Best Man** paired together.
- **The Bridesmaids and Groomsmen** paired together. Any extra Bridesmaids or Groomsmen can double-up, or may exit without an escort.
- **The Bride's Parents**
- **The Groom's Parents**
- **The Officiant**

Not every wedding service will contain all of these items, nor will they follow this exact order. Some couples want their wedding services to be short and sweet, while others prefer a lengthier, more traditional service. Because of this, many officiants will vary their services to suit a particular couple's needs. Certain religious ceremonies, on the other hand, must adhere to strict guidelines for their content and structure.

If you have the latitude to do so, there are many ways to personalize your wedding service. While tradition continues to be a significant factor in weddings, it is tradition with a twist. The following are some ideas that you may want to consider:

- As is customary in Jewish weddings, have both of your parents walk you down the aisle. The groom can participate in this custom too by starting the processional off by escorting his parents down the aisle.
- Walk down the aisle by yourself, or have your groom meet you halfway. You can also make a grand entrance as a couple and walk down the aisle together.
- Have a special song performed during the prelude or even during the processional or recessional. Pick a nontraditional wedding song— maybe your college alma mater if that is where you both met, or a theme song from a special movie or musical.
- Have your officiant read a special welcome written by you and your fiancé. If you are feeling bold, ask the officiant if the two of you can share the microphone to personally welcome your guests.
- Write your own vows. Make them as unique and as personal as you can.
- Incorporate special readings or songs into the ceremony. Involve special family members or friends by asking them to read a special selection. If they are talented, ask them to perform a song. The bride and groom can join in too (if they are not too nervous)!

Now that you have given some thought about what goes into a wedding ceremony, take the time to discuss your wedding service with your fiancé. Use the provided Ceremony Outline Worksheet (on page 169) to detail some of the decisions you have made regarding the ceremony. Couples who have the leeway to customize their ceremonies may have a full worksheet. On the other hand, couples who find that there is not much that they want or are allowed to change about the traditional wedding service may not find it necessary to fill out the entire worksheet.

When you are done creating the outline, make extra copies of it to give to your officiant. You can mail or fax a copy to him when it is complete, or present it to him in person during your final meeting (you will be scheduling this meeting during Weekend Six). If you have a wedding consultant or ceremony site coordinator who will be creating any itineraries for you, this person should also be sent a copy so that she can include any pertinent information about the ceremony in the master wedding day itinerary (see Chapter Six).

DEVELOP THE RECEPTION OUTLINE

(Sunday Afternoon)

By now you have already made most of the important arrangements necessary to create your version of the perfect wedding reception. You've reserved a wonderful location, you've selected the type of food and cake you will be serving, and you have great musical entertainment lined up. But as with many things in life, timing is the key! By developing a reception outline, you and your fiancé can set the pace for all of the activities that will take place during the postwedding celebration.

To get started, familiarize yourself with the major events that traditionally take place during a wedding reception:

The Cocktail Reception (Optional): Hors d'oeuvres and drinks can be served on trays or offered on a buffet in an area adjacent to where the meal will be served.

The Receiving Line (Optional): This is a way to ensure that you will be able to personally greet all of your guests. The line should be set up at the entrance of the dining area before your guests are invited to take their seats. A receiving line can also be set up at the back of the ceremony site, as your guests are filing out after the wedding service. Be sure to control the flow of the line by only sharing a few words with each person. Who participates in the receiving line is up to you, but typically it includes the following people in the following order:

- The Bride's Mother
- The Bride's Father
- The Groom's Mother
- The Groom's Father

- The Bride
- The Groom

The Grand Entrance: The master of ceremonies (the DJ, bandleader, etc.) will introduce and announce the entrance of the parents, the wedding party, and the newlyweds to their guests.

The Toast: The first toast is traditionally offered by the Best Man. Additional toasts can follow from other family members, friends, or the couple.

Meal Service: Guests will be served the meal at their table or may be invited to help themselves to a buffet or an assortment of food stations.

Greeting of the Guests (if there was no receiving line): The bride and groom can circulate from table to table to greet their guests.

The First Dance: The bride and groom dance together for the first time as husband and wife.

The Father/Daughter Dance: The bride will share a special dance with her father.

Dancing: All of your guests will be invited onto the dance floor to dance and have a good time.

The Cake Cutting Ceremony: With the groom's hand over the bride's, they will cut a piece from the bottom tier of the wedding cake—then feed it to each other. Afterward, the catering staff will cut and serve the cake to the guests.

The Bouquet Toss: All of the single female guests will be invited to assemble together. The bride will then turn her back to the group and throw her bouquet up in the air for someone to catch. The person who catches it is supposed to be the next in the group to get married.

The Garter Toss: All of the single male guests will be invited to gather around the groom, who will throw the bride's garter behind him for someone to catch. The man who catches the garter is supposed to be the next one to get married.

The Last Dance: The DJ or bandleader will invite everyone onto the dance floor for the final dance of the evening.

The Getaway: The bride and groom make a grand departure. Their guests can shower them with rose petals, bubbles, birdseed, etc., as they walk to and get into their car or other form of transportation.

There is no set rule dictating if and when any of the above activities must take place during your reception; however the listing above follows the most traditional ordering. When deciding what pacing works best for your celebration, there are many factors to take into consideration, including:

- The Time of Day: If your ceremony concludes close to a mealtime, you may want to offer the meal service as soon as possible, and save the other reception activities for later. This will ensure that your guests do not get too hungry.
- The Day of the Week: If your ceremony takes place on a weeknight or Sunday evening, you may want to schedule the cake cutting and other activities as soon as possible after the dinner service. This will ensure that your guests won't miss any special moments if they have to leave the reception early in order to be rested for work or any other commitments they may have the following morning.
- Photography and Videography Time Constraints: If your photographer or videographer is scheduled to leave before the end of the reception, you should schedule all of the important events that you want captured on film/tape before his departure.

For some creative ways to pace the fun and excitement of your wedding reception, we have included the following variations to the traditional wedding reception timetable:

DANCE, DANCE, DANCE!

(Follow this time line for a great way to get your guests involved right from the start. If you have a fun crowd, they'll love all the energy created by the continuous activity of dancing.)

- The Cocktail Reception (optional)
- The Receiving Line (optional)
- The Grand Entrance of the Parents, Wedding Party, and the Newlyweds
- The First Dance
- Dancing (All guests are invited onto the dance floor for one song.)
- The Toast
- First Course Served

- More Dancing (All guests are invited onto the dance floor for two songs as the plates are being cleared.)
- Dinner Service
- The Father/Daughter Dance
- Group Dance Greeting (This works great in addition to or in lieu of a receiving line. All of the guests will be invited onto the dance floor to share a dance with the bride and groom. The couple will navigate around the dance floor to greet all the guests, or the guests will be encouraged to "cut-in" and dance with the bride and groom for short intervals.)
- Dancing Continues
- The Cake Cutting Ceremony (After the bride and groom have cut the cake, a conga line can be formed. The dance should conclude by the cake table where the guests will be served a piece of cake as they dance by.)
- The Bouquet Toss
- The Garter Toss
- Dancing Continues
- The Last Dance (Everyone will be invited for one last group dance before the end of the evening. A large circle can be formed around the couple, and at the end of the song, everyone can come together in the middle to give the happy couple a warm group hug to send them on their way.)
- The Getaway

Keeping It Fresh!

(The following time line will also get your party started right away. Most of the events happen at the beginning of the reception, so the bride and groom will still look fresh for any wedding photographs. After the bouquet and garter toss, you can let your hair down and enjoy an uninterrupted block of dancing.)

- The Cocktail Reception (optional)
- The Receiving Line (optional)
- The Grand Entrance of the Parents, Wedding Party and the Newlyweds
- The Toast

- The First Dance
- The Father/Daughter Dance
- The Cake Cutting Ceremony (The cake will be brought back into the kitchen after the cake-cutting ceremony, and will be served by the catering staff after the meal.)
- The Meal Service
- The Greeting of the Guests (if there was no receiving line)
- The Bouquet Toss
- The Garter Toss
- A Continuous Block of Dancing!
- The Last Dance
- The Getaway

There are so many different memorable possibilities available when it comes to orchestrating a wedding reception. Today, more and more couples are taking up the challenge of creating their own variations on the traditional reception events. The most common events that get changed or deleted are the bouquet and garter toss. As couples are getting married later in life, this event seems to lose its appropriateness. The getaway often gets deleted from the reception itinerary as well, as many couples decide they want to enjoy every minute of the party they spent so long planning—and want to be the last ones to leave.

Take the time to collaborate with your fiancé about how you envision your perfect wedding reception unfolding. Use the Reception Outline Worksheet (see page 173) as a guide to devise the basic plan. When you are done, you can share a copy with your wedding consultant or reception site coordinator (if she will be helping you create the reception itinerary). About three weeks before the wedding, the completed worksheet will be your guide while constructing the reception portion of the master wedding day itinerary (see Chapter Six).

THE CALLIGRAPHER

Name of Company: _____

Contact's Name: _____

Phone: _____   Fax: _____

E-mail: _____

Address: _____

Date of Appointment: _____

QUESTIONS TO ASK

- How much do you charge?

- Is the rate per envelope? Per line? Per hour?

- Does the rate include addressing the inner envelopes as well? If not, how much will this service cost?

- Is there a minimum order that you require?

- What type of pen do you use?

- Do we have a choice of different ink colors?

- Do we have a choice of different printing styles?

- Can we see samples of your work?

- How much time do you need to address our envelopes?

- How many extra envelopes will you need?

- Will you assemble the invitations as well? If yes, is this included in the price?

- What type of accuracy guarantee do you have? What happens if I find mistakes?

- Will you redo them at no cost? How quickly can they be redone?

THE CALLIGRAPHER (CONT'D)

ADDITIONAL COMMENTS:

_____

_____

_____

_____

THE HAIR AND MAKEUP ARTIST

Name of Salon/Company: _____

Contact's Name: _____

Phone: _____ Fax: _____

E-mail: _____

Address: _____

Dates Available: _____

QUESTIONS TO ASK

- How much do you charge for hair styling?

- How much do you charge for makeup application?

- Is this rate per person or hourly?

- When is the full amount due? What method of payment do you prefer? (cash, check, credit card)

- Are gratuities included?

- Do you offer any discounts or group rates if my wedding party and family utilize your services as well?

- Will you come to our wedding site, or do we have to go to your salon? If you do come to the wedding site, will this involve any additional costs?

- What type of cosmetics do you use?

- Do we need to bring any of our own cosmetics the day of the wedding?

- Typically how long will the makeup last?

- What type of hair products do you use?

- Do we need to bring any of our own hair products, clips, bobby pins, or other accessories?

- Typically, for how long will the hair style hold up?

- Are there any special preparations necessary, such as washing my hair the night before?

- How much time should we allot for the hair and makeup process?

- What time should we get started the day of the wedding?

- If hair and makeup will be done on site, do you need any special equipment at the site, such as chairs, extension cords, mirrors, curling irons, hot rollers, hair dryers, extra lighting, etc.

- How much space do you need on site?

- Are you familiar with our wedding site? Do you need driving directions or a map?

- What beauty tips or maintenance advice do you suggest I follow before the wedding?

ADDITIONAL COMMENTS:

_____

_____

THE TRANSPORTATION COMPANY

Name of Company:

Contact's Name:

Driver's Name (if different from above):

Phone: Fax:

E-mail:

Address:

Dates Available:

QUESTIONS TO ASK

- What type of vehicle (make, model, year, and color) will you guarantee us on our wedding day?

- How many people can the vehicle comfortably accommodate?

- May we decorate the outside of the vehicle if we wish to?

- What does your rate include? How many hours of transportation?

- Are there any additional charges?

- Are gratuities included?

- What type of deposit is required?

- When is payment due in full? What method payment do you accept? (cash, check, credit card)

- Will any special "extras" be included such as a bottle of champagne or snacks in the vehicle?

- What time will you arrive to pick us up?

- What type of liability insurance does your company carry?

- If we run into any overtime on our wedding day, at what rate will we be charged?

- Are you familiar with our wedding ceremony and reception locations? Do you need a map or any driving directions?

ADDITIONAL COMMENTS:

_____

_____

_____

THE VALET PARKING COMPANY

Name of Company: _____

Contact's Name: _____

Phone: _____ Fax: _____

E-mail: _____

Address: _____

Dates Available: _____

QUESTIONS TO ASK

- Do you have experience working at our wedding and/or reception site?

- Are you familiar with the site's parking layout and restrictions? Can you adhere to them?

- What does your rate include? How many hours of service?

- Are gratuities included?

THE VALET PARKING COMPANY
(CONT'D)

- What type of deposit is required?

- When is payment due in full? What method of payment do you accept? (cash, check, credit card)

- What type of liability insurance does your company carry?

- What will your parking attendants be wearing on our wedding day?

ADDITIONAL COMMENTS:

_____

_____

_____

_____

THE CHILD CARE PROVIDER

Name of Company: _____

Contact's Name: _____

Care Provider's Name (if different from above): _____

Phone: _____ Fax: _____

E-mail: _____

Address: _____

Dates Available: _____

QUESTIONS TO ASK

- What is your hourly rate?

- With what ages of children do you have experience?

- How many children would you be comfortable taking care of on our wedding day?

- Are you familiar with our ceremony site and the space we have set up for the children?

- Do you need a map or any driving instructions?

- Will you need any special toys, games, or books for the children that day?

ADDITIONAL COMMENTS:

_____

_____

_____

_____

THE CEREMONY OUTLINE WORKSHEET

Place numbers in front of the following events according to the order you want them to take place. For example, if the Prelude will be the first order of business, place the number "1" in front of it. Do not put any numbers in front of activities that you do not want to include in your ceremony. Add any notes regarding the event on the lines provided. If needed, include any additional activities on the blank lines provided at the end of the list, and don't forget to include them in your numbering.

THE CEREMONY OUTLINE
WORKSHEET (cont'd)

_____ The Prelude: _____

_____ The Processional: (list names in order) _____

_____

_____

_____ The Welcome or Greeting: _____

_____ The Opening Readings and/or Prayers: _____

_____

_____ Musical Pieces and/or Solos: _____

_____

_____ The Giving Away/ Recognition of Parents: _____

_____

_____ The Charge to the Couple: _____

_____

_____ The Exchange of Vows: _____

_____

_____

_____

_____ The Ring Ceremony: _____

_____

_____ Prayers for the Couple/Thoughts on Marriage: _____

_____

_____ The Charge to the Guests: _____

_____

_____ Special Celebrations: _____

_____

_____ The Pronouncement: _____

_____ The Kiss: _____

_____ The Recessional: (list names in order)_____

      _____

      _____

      _____

ADDITIONAL ITEMS:

_____ _____

_____ _____

_____ _____

_____ _____

_____ _____

_____ _____

_____ _____

_____ _____

THE RECEPTION OUTLINE WORKSHEET

Place numbers in front of the following events according to the order you want them to take place. For example, if the cocktail reception will be the first order of business, place the number "1" in front of it. Do not put any numbers in front of activities that you do not want to include in your reception. Next to the number, within the parenthesis, place the approximate time that the event should take place. Add any notes regarding the event on the lines provided. If needed, include any additional activities on the blank

THE RECEPTION OUTLINE WORKSHEET (CONT'D)

lines provided at the end of the list, and don't forget to include them in your numbering.

_____ (:) The Cocktail Reception: _____

_____ (:) The Receiving Line: (list names of those participating in order) _____

_____

_____ (:) The Grand Entrance: (list names of those participating in order)

_____

_____ (:) The Toast: (list names of people performing toasts)

_____

_____ (:) Dinner Service: _____

_____

_____ (:) Greeting of the Guests: _____

_____ (:) The First Dance: (list name of song) _____

_____ (:) The Father/Daughter Dance: (list name of song) ____

_____ (:) Dancing: _____

_____ (:) The Cake Cutting: _____

_____ (:) The Bouquet Toss: _____

_____ (:) The Garter Toss: _____

_____ (:) The Last Dance: (list name of song) _____

_____ (:) The Getaway: _____

ADDITIONAL ITEMS:

_____ (:) _____

_____ (:) _____

_____ (:) _____

ADDITIONAL COMMENTS:

_____

_____

_____

_____

_____

_____

_____

_____

_____

_____

_____

_____

_____

_____

_____

_____

_____

_____

ADDITIONAL COMMENTS:

_____

_____

_____

_____

_____

_____

_____

_____

_____

_____

_____

_____

_____

_____

_____

_____

_____

_____

_____

_____

_____

_____

_____

_____

Weekend
Six
Checklist

☐ Obtain the Marriage License

☐ Have a Final Meeting with the Officiant

☐ Shop for the Wedding Accessories

☐ Prepare for the Final Dress Fitting

☐ Make Plans for the Rehearsal Dinner

☐ Shop for the Attendants' Gifts

OBTAIN THE
MARRIAGE LICENSE

(Friday Afternoon)

Obtaining a marriage license is one of the only wedding planning tasks that you and your fiancé are legally required to do. Depending on how far into the future the wedding date is, you may not be able to obtain the license this weekend. The requirements for obtaining a license vary from state to state, so there is no universal rule for how long a wedding license is valid. Typically, marriage licenses expire anywhere between sixty and ninety days from issuance, which means that you cannot get your license too far in advance of the actual wedding date.

At the very least, take the time to research the marriage license requirements for the state in which you will be married. Call the county Registrar's Office, or the office of the Recorder/Clerk, to find out what documents (driver's licenses, birth certificates, proofs of citizenship, proofs of divorce, blood test results, etc.) will be required, as well as the days and times that licenses are issued.

Many offices offer recorded information to which you can listen for answers to frequently asked questions. Also check out any state and county web sites, or regional bridal magazines, for additional information about obtaining a marriage license in the area where you will be wed.

You might want to consider utilizing a marriage license service. These services will save you time by taking care of all the details, for an additional fee.

To obtain a marriage license if you will be married out of state or out of country, you will most likely be required either to plan a weekday trip to the area or to arrive at your destination a few days prior to the ceremony. If you choose the latter, be sure to arrive far enough in advance to fulfill any waiting period requirements.

Once you have obtained the license, keep it in a safe place and don't forget to bring it along with you on the wedding day. Your officiant, your witnesses, and you and your new husband may all be required to sign it after the wedding service has taken place. It is usually the officiant's responsibility to then send the signed copy back to the appropriate government office as a legal record that the marriage took place. Just be sure to follow the filing instructions provided with the license. If you think that you might forget to bring the license to the ceremony, give it to the Best Man or your officiant on the day of the rehearsal.

HAVE A FINAL MEETING WITH THE OFFICIANT

(Friday Evening)

If your officiant does not require any additional meetings with you and your fiancé before the wedding rehearsal, you can skip this section altogether. Just be sure that he has received a copy of the Ceremony Outline Worksheet (see page 171), and does not have any further questions or comments about it.

However, some officiants require multiple meetings with couples before the wedding day, mainly to discuss specifics about the service and to perform premarital counseling. Now that the majority of your wedding planning is taken care of, take this opportunity to get together with your officiant and discuss any questions or concerns that you have about the marriage ceremony or your future roles as husband and wife.

SHOP FOR THE WEDDING ACCESSORIES

(Saturday Morning)

There are many accessories that work together to create your wedding's style. If you have not already purchased all of your wedding accessories, have fun while venturing out on this important shopping spree. The following are some items you might still need to consider purchasing or borrowing for the wedding day.

For the Bride

- Veil, Headpiece, or Other Hair Accessories
- Shoes
- Jewelry
- Lingerie
- Hosiery
- Gloves
- Garter
- Handkerchief
- Purse
- Something "Old"
- Something "New"
- Something "Borrowed"
- Something "Blue"

For the Wedding Party

- Shoes
- Jewelry
- Hosiery
- Gloves
- Decorative Pillow or Box for the Ring Bearer
- Decorative Basket for the Flower Girl

Wedding Accessories and Decor

- Guest Book
- Pen for the Guest Book
- Toasting Goblets
- Cake Knife and Server
- Unity Candle
- Aisle Runner
- Card Box for the Gift Table
- Place Cards
- Table Numbers
- Disposable Cameras for Guest Tables

There are a few things to keep in mind when shopping for certain wedding accessories. When looking for a veil or headpiece, try to find one that not only complements the style of your wedding dress but also nicely frames your face and works well with the wedding day hairstyle you have selected.

The shoes you wear are also an important accessory—not only because of the way they look but also because of the way they will make you feel. You may be on your feet for upward of twelve hours on the wedding day, so comfort should be a factor. Some brides even select two pairs of shoes, one pair being a more formal shoe for the ceremony, and the other a more comfortable dancing shoe for the reception. No matter how many pairs of shoes you decide to bring with you, be sure to break them in as much as possible before the actual wedding day.

If your attendants do not already have all of the necessary accessories to complete their wedding ensembles, at this time you may want to purchase some of the above listed items for them as well. Before heading out, make sure you know all of your attendants' shoe and hosiery sizes. Bring along the Wedding Party Roster (see page 49) for easy reference to this information.

If you want to save the time and hassle of driving from store to store, there are many bridal salons, wedding planning and resource centers, and catalogs that carry everything a bride and her wedding party could need. The prices may be slightly higher at these one-stop shops, but you will be able to completely accessorize your wedding during one giant shopping excursion. This is a great help for any busy bride!

PREPARE FOR THE FINAL DRESS FITTING

(Saturday Afternoon) (Optional)

If your wedding dress is being custom-made, or if you have ordered your dress from a salon, you may need to attend a final dress fitting. This visit will ensure that your dress fits as perfectly as possible, and will also be a good opportunity to make any last-minute adjustments to its look or style.

The date the wedding dress will be finished will determine whether or not you can schedule the fitting to actually take place this weekend, or will only be able to make the necessary preparations for it to occur at a later date.

The first step toward preparing for the dress fitting is to call ahead and make an appointment with your dressmaker or salon salesperson. To guarantee that the fitting is accurate and beneficial, it is essential to bring along the following items:

- **Your Wedding Shoes:** Absolutely necessary for determining the proper hemline of the gown!
- **Your Wedding Lingerie:** Wear these items during the fitting to make sure that they "do" what they need to do (i.e., lift, tuck, enhance, support, or conceal where needed).
- **Your Headpiece, Veil, Jewelry, Gloves, or Other Bridal Accessories:** Try all these accessories on with your dress to get a feel for how the entire outfit works together.
- **A Family Member or Bridal Party Member:** Bring someone along with you who can learn the proper way to bustle your gown's train (if you have one). This will definitely be a great help to you on the wedding day. Bustling a train is not something you can do by yourself.

MAKE PLANS FOR THE REHEARSAL DINNER

(Saturday Afternoon and/or Sunday Morning)

The rehearsal dinner is a great opportunity for you and your fiancé to spend time with your wedding party, family, and friends in a more intimate and relaxed setting than your wedding reception. The meal is held immediately after the rehearsal, which means that it can also be a breakfast, or a luncheon, if the rehearsal is held during the day. Traditionally, the groom's family pays for the expense, though it is often the bride and groom who choose the location and make most of the arrangements.

The following people should be invited to the rehearsal dinner:

- The immediate families of the bride and groom
- All members of the wedding party, their spouses or significant others, and their children (if they have traveled from out of town)
- Any children in the wedding party, and their parents
- The officiant and his spouse
- Any family members who have traveled from out of town (this is optional if budget or space restrictions apply)
- Any friends who have traveled from out of town (this is optional if budget or space restrictions apply)

Selecting a location for your rehearsal dinner depends on how many people you will be inviting, the formality, the dinner menu, the budget, and the proximity of the restaurant from the rehearsal site. If you are unfamiliar with restaurants in the area, get recommendations from your wedding consultant or site coordinator, and then sample a meal or a few appetizers at the top choices. When you are there, ask the management to show you exactly where in the establishment they will be able to accommodate a group of your size. For a more casual event, many couples choose to prepare the meals themselves, or arrange for catering, at a nearby home, park, or even at the beach.

Once you have decided on a location and have made all the necessary arrangements (reservations, menu selection, deposit paid, etc.), it's a nice idea to send invitations to everyone invited to the rehearsal dinner. Mail the invitations about two weeks beforehand. For any wedding party members, parents, or other people playing a role in your ceremony or reception, include their invitation with the confirmation package that you will be creating during Chapter Seven.

SHOP FOR THE ATTENDANTS' GIFTS

(Sunday Afternoon and/or Evening)

Presenting your attendants with gifts the day of the rehearsal, or at some other special time prior to the wedding day, is a nice way to let your wedding party know just how much you appreciate their involvement in the wedding.

Discuss with your fiancé what types of gifts you would like to present to your wedding party, and agree upon a budget for the purchases. Discuss whether you will be presenting identical gifts to the groomsmen and bridesmaids, unique gifts for each individual member of the wedding party, or two different types of gifts—one type for each of the bridesmaids and one type for each of the groomsmen. Be thoughtful and creative with your purchases, and know that there are no set rules for the gifts you give to your attendants. Some ideas include:

For Everyone

- Gift Certificates (from a specialty store, catalog, day spa, or restaurant)
- Tickets (to a play, concert, or sporting event)
- Books
- CDs
- Jewelry
- Magazine Subscriptions
- Gift Baskets (with exotic bath products, unique foods and kitchen supplies, or anything fun!)
- Monogrammed Bath Robes
- Picture Frames

For Her

- Matching Purses (in the same or different colors)
- Decorative Hair Accessories
- A Beautiful Wrap or Scarf
- A Tote or Makeup Bag Full of Beauty Supplies

For Him

- Engraved Pens, Money Clips, Business Card Holders, or Mugs
- Sporting Equipment
- Tools for the Barbecue
- Collectible Comic Books, Action Figures, Model Cars, or Other Fun Toys

Don't forget to include gifts for any children in the wedding, or for any other people who will be performing a special service or helping out, such as the "Troubleshooter," the guest book attendant, the greeters, or the readers. Many couples also choose to present their parents with special gifts of appreciation and love.

Lastly, decide if you and your fiancé will be exchanging gifts with each other on the wedding day. When shopping for your future spouse, try to find something that will forever remind both of you of the joy you shared on your special day. Some ideas include:

For Each Other

- Jewelry
- Decorative or Unique Jewelry Boxes to Hold the New Wedding Rings
- A Book of Romantic Poetry or Photographs with a Special Inscription on the Inside Cover
- Beautiful Artwork
- A Framed Photograph of You Two on Your First Date, or a Framed Copy of an Early Love Letter or Card
- A Box Set of Romantic Music CDs or Movies
- A Special Outfit to Wear on the Honeymoon
- Luggage and a Promise to See the World Together

THE MARRIAGE LICENSE

Name of Government Office/Company: _____

Contact's Name: _____

Phone: _____   Fax: _____

E-mail: _____

Address: _____

THE MARRIAGE LICENSE (CONT'D)

QUESTIONS TO ASK

- What type of documents do we need to bring with us to obtain our license?

- Do we need to apply in person? Do we both have to appear at the same time?

- On what days, and during what hours, can we obtain our license? What days and times are the least busy at your office?

- Is there any office where we can obtain our license after business hours or on weekends?

- Can we make an appointment?

- Are any blood tests required?

- How long will the process take? What does the process entail?

- Are there any residency or citizenship requirements?

- How much does the license cost? Are there different types of licenses at different costs (public, confidential)?

- What type of payment do you accept?

- Is there a waiting period before the license is valid?

- How long after issuance will the license remain valid?

- I am getting married at (fill in the name of ceremony site). This license will be valid there, correct?

ADDITIONAL COMMENTS:

_____

_____

_____

_____

THE REHEARSAL DINNER

Name of Facility/Restaurant: _____

Contact's Name: _____

Phone: _____   Fax: _____

E-mail: _____

Address: _____

Dates Available: _____

QUESTIONS TO ASK

- Do you have facilities appropriate for holding a rehearsal dinner?

- Are there any private rooms or areas available at your facility?

- What is the maximum and minimum number of guests you can accommodate?

- Do you have special group menus or can my guests choose from any of the menu items?

- What is the price range for your meals?

- Is there ample parking available? At what cost?

- How many servers will you provide for a group our size?

- May we come in and sample your menu?

- What type of deposit is required to hold the space?

- When is the payment due in full?

- How soon in advance do I have to guarantee a seat count?

- Do you offer vegetarian meals, and other special dietary requests?

- How long can my group stay at your establishment? Are you expecting any other large groups after us? At the same time?

THE REHEARSAL DINNER (CONT'D)

ADDITIONAL COMMENTS:

_____

_____

BEYOND THE
SIX WEEKENDS

Congratulations! You have now completed the majority of your wedding planning, and can look forward to resuming the life you once knew. You remember—the life where you actually socialized or just relaxed on the weekends.

If you have successfully accomplished all of the goals set forth in the Six-Weekend Wedding Planner, you can safely put this book aside and not open it up again until three weeks before the wedding. If you have the time, you may want to read ahead anyway to get a head start. The remaining chapters will walk you through some last minute preparations essential to organizing and executing the perfect wedding day and honeymoon.

For those of you who have enjoyed the planning process so much that you don't want to stop, or for those who have discovered there is still more to do to fulfill your vision of "wedding perfection," we are leaving you with a few items that can be turned into additional weekend goals, if you so desire.

ADDITIONAL WEEKEND GOALS (OPTIONAL)
- ☐ Take Dance Lessons
- ☐ Make or Purchase Wedding Favors
- ☐ Make or Purchase Additional Wedding Decorations or Accessories
- ☐ Make Wedding Programs
- ☐ Make Menu Cards for Reception Tables
- ☐ Frame Engagement Photo or Other Special Photos for Display at Wedding
- ☐ Make or Purchase Gift Baskets for the Out-of-Town Guests

6

Creating the Final Game Plan

As "the day" approaches, you will realize just how much you have accomplished in the previous weeks or months. You have hired caterers and florists, tasted cakes, and purchased the gown of your dreams. After all of your hard work and careful planning, it would be a shame for anyone, or anything, to fall through the cracks. Don't let this happen to you! Three weeks before the wedding date begin the final stage of planning.

ORGANIZE A COMPLETE ITINERARY FOR THE "BIG DAY"

So many details. So many people. How can you manage all this and not have a riot break out? People work best with structure, and that is exactly what needs to be in place to avoid wedding chaos.

Establishing an itinerary for the wedding day is essential to ensure that the day runs as smoothly and as close to schedule as possible. In Weekend Five, you have already determined which activities and events will be a part of your ceremony and reception, as well as established a time line for these events. Here, you will complete the puzzle of the wedding day by creating a complete itinerary that will ensure everyone involved has a written guide that describes exactly how the wedding day will unfold.

If you have hired a wedding consultant, she may already be working on an itinerary. If you are preparing the itinerary yourself, consult with your officiant or ceremony site coordinator when developing it. If either offers to organize an itinerary for you, ask for a copy and review it with your fiancé before giving the final OK. Talk to the officiant or site coordinator if there are any adjustments or corrections that you deem necessary.

These are the steps for organizing a wedding day itinerary:

1. Find out what time the site is open and available to your wedding party and your vendors.

2. Determine where you and your bridesmaids will be dressing. The same goes for the groom and his groomsmen. Many hotels offer a hospitality room to the wedding party. Some churches offer a changing room. Others prefer to prepare for the day at their home or their parent's home.

3. Determine how long it will take you and your bridesmaids to have your hair and/or makeup done, as well as dress for the wedding. The bride should be one of the last to have her hair and makeup done, as it is important to keep the bride looking fresh. Allow plenty of time to prepare.

4. Determine when you are going to take photographs. Will you see the groom before the ceremony and use this opportunity to take the majority of your photos, or will the two of you take your photos together after the ceremony? Whichever you choose, account for that time. Should you take your photos preceremony, talk to your photographer and allot the proper amount of time to complete the photo session. If you take photos between the ceremony and reception, this will require allotting additional time between the two events.

5. Gather all vendors' phone numbers, pager numbers, and names of the contact persons.

6. Map out and determine the order of the day. Confirm at what time the vendors will be able to arrive at the appropriate site. Have the order

make sense. (For example, you will want to have your personal flowers delivered before the photographer begins taking photos.)

7. If certain vendors, like the photographer, videographer, or disc jockey are hired on a per-hour basis, take this into account. For example, if the photographer's package includes five hours of time, you will want him to cover the important aspects of the wedding—the ceremony, the toast, the first dance, the cake cutting, etc. If the wedding begins at 5:00 P.M., don't ask the photographer to arrive at 1:00 P.M., and expect to get all the aforementioned covered. He'll be gone right after the ceremony.

8. Take travel time into account, whether it be from your home to the ceremony and/or the ceremony to the reception. If the weather is expected to be inclement, take this into account. Don't forget about traffic. Although traffic in certain areas is unpredictable, about two weeks before, take a drive to and around the ceremony and reception site at the same time, on the same day of the week, to get a feel for the amount of traffic in the area. You may want to check for any road construction in the area as well.

9. Delays do occur and some people are just always late. Consider whether or not it will be comforting to you if you pad the arrival times for the wedding party, family, or vendors to account for tardiness.

Though at first it may seem like a lot of work to put together an itinerary, you will be glad that you did. The itinerary works as a guideline for how you and your fiancé want the events to progress throughout the day. With all the information clearly indicated on the itinerary, your wedding vendors, family members, and wedding party will have no questions about who needs to be where, and when they need to be there. You will be freed from answering the same questions over and over, and will be able to enjoy the celebration of your new status as husband and wife!

See the following pages for a sample Wedding Day Itinerary based on the following information:

A 4:00 P.M. start time with the ceremony and reception being held at the same location. Most photos will be taken before the ceremony, including the bride and groom together.

SAMPLE WEDDING DAY ITINERARY

Keep in mind that every wedding schedule is unique. The following is a simplified wedding day itinerary. Your own itinerary would contain specific names and contact information. As well, the times would be adjusted to fit your wedding day timetable.

BETTY BRIDE AND GREGORY GROOM'S WEDDING DAY ITINERARY

SATURDAY, JULY 1, 2000

11:15 A.M.
- Wendy Wedding (the wedding consultant) arrives.

11:30 A.M.
- Bride and bridesmaids arrive at location.
- Hair and makeup artists arrive.

1:30 P.M.
- The groom and groomsmen arrive at location ALREADY dressed.
- Mother of the bride arrives to have her hair and makeup done.
- Florist arrives. She distributes personal flowers, decorates ceremony site, then decorates reception area.
- "Boxed" lunch is served (arranged by Wendy Wedding).

1:45 P.M.
- Photographer arrives.

2:00 P.M.
- Catering staff arrives to begin setup. (Site must be ready by 3:30 P.M.)
- Rental equipment arrives and is set up by the catering staff.
- The bride, groom, and members of the wedding party must be ready for pictures.
- Private photo session begins with the bride and groom.

2:30 P.M.

- Bride's and groom's immediate families arrive for photos.
- Baker arrives to set up cake.

3:00 P.M.

- Ceremony musicians arrive and set up. Must be complete by 3:30 P.M. (before guests arrive).
- DJ arrives and sets up for reception. Must be complete by 4:30 P.M.
- Officiant arrives.
- Child care provider arrives.
- Valet parking staff arrives.

3:15 P.M.

- Finish taking photos.
- Bride, groom, and wedding party retire to respective rooms.

3:30 P.M.

- Musicians begin playing.
- Parents of the bride and groom greet guests as they arrive.
- Groomsmen:
    - A. Direct guests to sign the guest book.
    - B. When applicable, advise guests that child care is available for young children.
    - C. Escort guests to their seats

4:00 P.M.

- Show Time!!!
- Bride's grandparents are escorted to their seats.
- Groom's grandparents are escorted to their seats.
- The officiant takes his position.
- The groom takes his position.
- Groom's parents are escorted to their seats.
- Bride's mother is escorted to her seat.
- The processional begins.
- The wedding party walks down the aisle in the designated order.
- The Wedding March begins.
- The bride, escorted by her father, walks down the aisle.

BETTY BRIDE AND GREGORY GROOM'S WEDDING DAY (CONT'D)

- Bride's father takes his seat.
- Ceremony continues under officiant's direction.

4:45 P.M.
- The ceremony ends and the wedding party regroups for additional photos.
- The guests are invited to enjoy cocktails and hors d'oeuvres.
- The ceremony musicians play cocktail music during this time.

5:45 P.M.
- Guests are invited into the dining room for the reception.
- The DJ plays music as the guests are seated.

6:00 P.M.
- The Grand Entrance
- DJ introduces the parents of the bride and groom.
- DJ introduces the wedding party.
- (Music selection changes.)
- DJ introduces the bride and groom as "Mr. and Mrs. . . ."
- DJ invites the best man to toast the bride and groom.

6:15 P.M.
- The first course is served.
- The DJ plays soft dinner music.

6:45 P.M.
- Bride and groom greet guests at their tables.

7:15 P.M.
- DJ announces the first dance. Bride and groom dance.
- Immediately after the first dance, DJ asks the bride and her father to the dance floor for the father/daughter dance.
- The groom and his mother join the bride and her father halfway through the song.
- The wedding party proceeds to the dance floor.

- Guests are invited to join the bride, groom, and wedding party on the dance floor.

8:00 P.M.
- DJ directs guests' attention to the cake cutting. Cake is served to the guests.
- Dancing continues.

8:30 P.M.
- DJ invites all the single women to participate in the bouquet toss.
- DJ invites single men to participate in the garter toss.

9:30 P.M.
- Dancing continues.
- Groomsmen assist in loading the gifts into designated car.

9:55 P.M.
- DJ asks the guests to join the bride and groom on the dance floor for the last dance.

10:00 P.M.
- The bride and groom make their grand departure as newlyweds and live happily ever after!!!

ORGANIZE
THE REHEARSAL

Now that you have established the sequence of events for the wedding day, organizing the rehearsal is relatively quick and easy. If you are working with a wedding consultant, she will work with you to develop a plan of attack for the rehearsal. You will need to consult with your officiant and the site coordinator before finalizing any plans. The church or site may have rules or regulations that must be followed. In this case, work with the appropriate person/persons to establish a working order with which you feel comfortable. Ultimately this is your rehearsal and your wedding, and any comments, questions, or concerns you have should be addressed by one of these professionals.

The rehearsal is serious business, as it is the first and only chance to practice and run through the events of the wedding day. The ultimate goal of the rehearsal is to give the wedding party and family members, as well as you and your fiancé, an opportunity to get acquainted with your roles and positions for the following day. A well-run rehearsal will help calm your nerves and reassure you that things will work on the wedding day.

Generally, rehearsals are held the evening before the wedding, which is usually a Friday night. Since most weddings are held on the weekends, this gives out-of-towners the opportunity to arrive in town and attend the rehearsal without missing too much work. However, with the increasing popularity of "off-night" weddings, the site may be occupied the evening before. In this case, work with the site coordinator and your officiant to determine the best time to plan the rehearsal. For a Saturday wedding, a Thursday afternoon, or Friday morning rehearsal is an option as well.

If you have hired a wedding consultant, her services most likely include directing the rehearsal. In this case, once you review and finalize the itinerary, on the rehearsal night you can relax . . . a little. It will be the consultant's responsibility to tell your bridesmaids to be quiet or your soon-to-be mother-in-law where to sit. If you do not have a wedding consultant, work with the officiant or site coordinator to determine who will run the ceremony. In some instances, it may be necessary for you or the designated "Troubleshooter" to run the rehearsal. If this is the case, we provide instructions on how to do this later in the chapter.

Once the details, such as the date and time of the rehearsal and the rehearsal dinner location, are finalized, you should let involved friends, family members, and the wedding party know as soon as possible. Create a simple one-page document that includes the following information:

- The name of the bride and groom
- The date, time, and location for the rehearsal
- An overview of events at the rehearsal
- Location of the restaurant/location of the rehearsal dinner
- Brief overview of events for the wedding day

Send the rehearsal itinerary, along with the invitation for the rehearsal dinner and the checklist of what to bring (see page 211), in the confirmation package that you will be creating in Chapter Seven.

See the following Sample Rehearsal Itinerary.

SAMPLE REHEARSAL ITINERARY BETTY BRIDE AND GREGORY GROOM'S WEDDING REHEARSAL

6:00 P.M., FRIDAY, JUNE 30, 2000

MASSIVE MANSION—1313 SNOOTY LANE—HOLLYWOOD, CA

6:00 P.M.
- Meet on the front lawn of mansion.
- Introduce wedding consultant who will pass out wedding day itineraries. Consultant will direct the rehearsal. **Listen to her!**
- Bride, groom, and wedding party will practice their roles for the ceremony, under the consultant's direction.

7:00 P.M.
- Head over to restaurant for dinner! Don't forget your directions.

BRIEF OUTLINE OF EVENTS FOR SATURDAY JULY 1

11:30 A.M.: All bridesmaids must be at mansion for hair and makeup.

1:30 P.M.: Groom and groomsmen must be dressed and at mansion.

Lunch is served.

2:00 P.M.: Pictures begin—bride, groom, and wedding party must be dressed.

2:30 P.M.: Parents and other family members arrive for pictures.

3:30 P.M.: Guests begin arriving.

BETTY BRIDE AND GREGORY GROOM'S WEDDING REHEARSAL (CONT'D)

4:00 P.M.: Ceremony begins.

4:45 P.M.: Cocktail hour begins. Bride, groom, and wedding party regroup for more photos.

6:00 P.M.: Reception begins with Grand Entrance.

6:15 P.M.: Dinner is served.

9:55 P.M.: Last dance.

GROOMSMEN—DON'T FORGET . . .

- The items on the enclosed checklist (*make copies of the checklist on page 211*), including, tuxedo, dress shoes, black dress socks, and white undershirts.

BRIDESMAIDS—DON'T FORGET . . .

- The items on the enclosed checklist (*make copies of the checklist on page 211*), including the dress, shoes, jewelry, and appropriate lingerie.
- Lipstick that you want to wear on the wedding day.
- Any hair accessories you want to use.
- If you are getting your hair done, wash it the night before. The hair stylist prefers this when doing up-do's.

THE DO-IT-YOURSELF REHEARSAL

If you will be directing the rehearsal yourself, you will need to develop a more detailed itinerary. Your document should include the order of the rehearsal and all of the steps that need rehearsing, including who stands where and walks up or down the aisle with whom. You can do this by creating a new document, using the itinerary you sent out to your attendants as a template, or just handwrite notes for yourself directly onto the preexisting itinerary sheet.

Things to discuss or point out at the rehearsal include the following:

1. The standing positions for the bride, groom, officiant, and wedding party for the ceremony
2. Who will walk the parents down the aisle and where they will be sitting
3. Recessional order for the wedding party
4. Processional order for the wedding party
5. Reception Grand Entrance lineup for the wedding party
6. Reminders for the wedding party:
   - No gum chewing
   - No fidgeting during the ceremony
   - No whispering during the ceremony
   - Everyone should stand up straight and smile. Groomsmen keep their hands at their sides or behind their backs—NOT clasped in front or in pockets.
   - At what point the maid of honor takes the bride's bouquet during the ceremony
   - How ushers are to escort guests to their seats—offer their right arm to the female guest
   - How the groomsmen are to escort the bridesmaids during the processional and recessional—link arms, or bridesmaid takes hold of groomsman's bent arm, or walk side-by-side, or walk alone
   - Walk naturally, no locked steps or fancy footwork

In all the excitement, make sure you don't forget to bring the following items to the rehearsal: the ribbon bouquet (created from the bows and ribbons off of bridal shower gifts), copies of the wedding day itineraries (one for each person), and extra copies of maps and/or directions to the rehearsal dinner location.

If you will be running the rehearsal yourself, use the following sample of the Do-It-Yourself Rehearsal Itinerary to guide you in creating your own rehearsal itinerary. You will need to use the ceremony time line you established in Weekend Five, as well as talk to your officiant to complete this itinerary.

Please see the following sample of the Do-It-Yourself Rehearsal Itinerary.

SAMPLE DO-IT-YOURSELF REHEARSAL ITINERARY

6:00 P.M.

- Meet at rear lawn of mansion
- Make introductions and pass out wedding day itineraries
- Assume standing positions at front of ceremony site
    Bridesmaids to the left, from closest to the bride (Maid of Honor)
    to farthest away (**Insert names and order**)

_____

_____

_____

_____

_____

Groomsmen to the right, from closest to the groom (Best Man)
to farthest away (**Insert names and order**)

_____

_____

_____

_____

Officiant takes his place front and center
Bride and groom face officiant
Officiant will outline wedding ceremony
(**Insert ceremony timeline**)

_____

- Practice recessional, beginning with the bride and groom. (Quick, happy walk) **(Insert names in descending order)**

_____

_____

_____

_____

_____

_____

- Practice lineup for processional.
  A. Groom's parents **(Insert names)** escorted by **(Insert name of usher)**

  _____

  _____

  B. Bride's mother **(Insert name)** escorted by **(Insert name of usher)**

  _____

  C. Bridesmaids and groomsmen, starting with position farthest from the bride, and finishing with the Maid of Honor and Best Man. **(Insert names and order)**

  _____

  _____

  _____

  _____

  _____

SAMPLE DO-IT-YOURSELF REHEARSAL (CONT'D)

D. Flower girl and ring bearer (**Insert names**)

_____

_____

E. Bride escorted by her father

- Walk-through of processional (slow paced walk), taking positions in front of ceremony site again
- Quick review of ceremony (remind Maid of Honor when to take your bouquet)
- Go through list of wedding party reminders (see page 199)
- Walk through recessional one last time
- Practice lineup for reception grand entrance

A. Groom's parents (**Insert names**), enter and take seats

_____

B. Bride's parents (**Insert names**), enter and take seats

_____

C. Groomsmen and bridesmaids (**Insert names and order**), enter and take seats at head table

_____

D. The bride and groom (**Insert desired announcement**), enter and take seats at head table

_____

E. Best Man offers a toast

- Go over instructions for the wedding party dance, and any other duties of the bridesmaids and groomsmen for the next evening, such as loading gifts into the appropriate car, and participating in the evening's activities and dancing to keep the party going
- Make sure everyone has directions to the restaurant, and head over there

7

Ready, Set . . .
Two Weeks to Go!

The day you have been preparing for and waiting for is almost here. Finally, you are about to see the fruits of your labor, but there is still work to be done. These final two weeks before the wedding are crucial. Now is the time to pull it all together—all the vendors, all the details, and all the people.

CONFIRM THE DETAILS

The "big day" is quickly approaching. There are many details to firm up and pass along to the involved parties. About two weeks before the wedding is a good time to confirm plans and go over the details one final time. There is a lot of information you need to share not only with the wedding party and your families, but with all of your vendors as well.

Go through the information you have accumulated in your Portable Planner one last time to make sure everything is in order. You will be taking this to the wedding with you, where you will pass it along to your wedding consultant (of course, she will already be prepared) or your designated "Troubleshooter." They will use this as a guide for the day, and to confirm each vendor has fulfilled his end of the agreement.

The Vendors

To confirm details with your vendors, a letter followed up by a phone call is always best. Around this time, you will also be making final payments to your vendors. Should you wish to make any last-minute changes, now is the time to discuss it, do it, and pay for it. You will need to supply a final guest count to the reception facility (or caterer), the baker, the rental company, and possibly the ceremony facility at this time.

With this information in place, put together a "confirmation package," including a confirmation letter, directions, and any other necessary information. Mail or fax this package to the vendor. Always call the vendors three or four days later to verbally confirm receipt of the package. If you are working with a wedding consultant, she may be taking care of many of these details for you.

The confirmation letter should be concise but thorough. It should include (or reiterate) the pertinent information for each vendor. Other information to include with the confirmation letter includes:

- A map to the ceremony and/or reception location
- A copy of the complete itinerary with the information pertaining to that particular vendor highlighted for easy reference
- Contact person and phone number of the site coordinator or the site representative at the ceremony and reception locations
- A copy of the floor plan (if pertinent to the vendor's services)

Please see the following page for a sample confirmation letter.

Sample Confirmation Letter

June 18, 2000
Fanny's Fancy Photography
1818 Main Street
I Do, California 90273

Dear Fanny,

This is a letter confirming the details for the wedding of Betty Bride and Gregory Groom on Saturday, July 1, 2000. As per our conversation on June 10, please note the following time changes for photos:

- Photos will begin at 2:00 P.M.
- We will be taking bride and groom photos preceremony.
- As our ceremony begins at 4:00 P.M., I would like to have the preceremony photos of the bride and the bridesmaids completed by 3:15 P.M.

From your studio, travel time should be about thirty minutes to the Massive Mansion. Following is the address and telephone number of the mansion. I have enclosed a map as well. Please call if you have any questions.

Massive Mansion
1313 Snooty Lane
Hollywood, California 90845
(213) 555-0471
Site Contact: Gracious Owner

When you arrive at Massive Mansion, please check in with my wedding consultant, Wendy Wedding (pager number 213-555-0999). (She has blond hair and will be wearing a black floral dress.)

I look forward to working with you on July 1, 2000. I have included a copy of the wedding day itinerary so that you will know the sequence of events. I will call you in a few days to discuss this information further.

Sincerely,

Betty Bride

Enc.: Map
    Wedding Day Itinerary

The Wedding Party, Family Members, and Others Involved

Keeping the wedding party and involved family members abreast of the time line of events is important. At the same time you are sending out the vendors' "confirmation package," send out a similar type of package to the wedding party, family members, and any others on your "wedding day team." These letters should have a less formal tone.

Information to include in the confirmation package is as follows:

- Rehearsal Itinerary (see page 200), including the time each person will need to arrive at the appropriate site and/or be ready for photos on the wedding day. You may want to highlight this information so that it will not be overlooked.
- Map to the rehearsal location
- Approximate travel time to the site from various geographical areas
- Invitation to the rehearsal dinner, including the address, phone number, and a map to the location
- Checklist of things to bring on the wedding day (see page 211)

DEVELOP RECEPTION SEATING CHARTS

The response cards are in, the day is drawing closer, and now you have to decide where to seat all of these guests at the reception. After all, part of a successful wedding is the happiness of your special friends and family. A seating plan can alleviate any apprehension or embarrassment guests may feel if they must search to find an empty seat at a table. The task may seem trying and tedious, but taking the time to develop a seating plan shows you care.

Before you begin a seating plan for the guests, you need to make some basic decisions. First, you will need a copy of the floor plan for the reception. Your caterer, wedding consultant, or site coordinator will be able to provide you with this information. Then, you will need to decide where you and the groom will be seated. Whatever arrangement you choose, the table should be in a position that is visible to most of the room; after all, the guests are there to see you and your new husband.

Your seating choices include:

- **Head Table:** A long rectangular table placed at the front or focal point of the room. The bride and groom are seated at the center of the table, with the bride usually on the groom's right. The wedding party is seated on either side of them. The wedding party may be seated male/female or with all the bridesmaids on the bride's side, and the groomsmen on the groom's side.
- **Sweetheart Table:** The bride and groom are seated at a smaller table for just the two of them. The table is at the front or focal point of the room. The wedding party is then seated close to the sweetheart table, either with their spouses or dates, at a table with other members of the wedding party, or sitting throughout the room with family and friends. They do not need to all sit together.
- **Regular Seating:** The bride and groom are seated at a regular table toward the front or focal point of the room. The other people at the table may include their parents, siblings, grandparents, the officiant (and his spouse), and the Maid/Matron of Honor or the Best Man. Seat the wedding party as you would with a sweetheart table arrangement.

Once you have decided this, the next task is to consider where to seat your parents. The bride's and groom's parents may be seated at a table together, or each may "host" their own table. In the case of divorces and remarriages, it is a good idea for each parent to "host" their own table. The officiant (and his spouse) is usually seated with the bride's parents. The parents' table(s) should be in close proximity to the bride and groom's table. You may also want to place close relatives or friends at the parents' tables. Sitting with the parents is considered to be an honor.

Once you, your parents, and the wedding party have been assigned seats, you need to concentrate on the remaining guests. It is not necessary to seat only family around the bride and groom. You may choose to seat close friends near your table. It is also not necessary to have the bride's family and friends on one side and the groom's on the other. This is a marriage of not only two people but also two families, and two sets of friends. Mix the tables so that the room is not divided.

When assigning tables to the guests, be considerate. Try to arrange the seating so that those guests with similar interests, personalities, or careers will be seated together. This gives a starting point for comfortable conversation. If you are not familiar with the interests of some of your parents' guests, ask them for this information. Also ask if they have any suggestions about with whom they should be seated. If certain family members do not get along with other family members, seat them on opposite ends of the room. Between you and your fiancé, you should be able to "read" your guests and make an educated decision that will please everyone (almost).

You may also want to consider mixing single guests with married or escorted guests at tables. Having a table for singles only may look like a set-up and cause discomfort for the single guests. In the case of the spouses and/or escorts of the wedding party, they may be seated at one table near the wedding party or dispersed throughout the tables. Seating them together has its advantages. First of all, they will have something in common, and since it is the job of the wedding party to keep the wedding lively, they will most likely be out on the dance floor and involved in the other reception activities.

Once you have designated tables for the guests at your wedding, you will need to decide how to direct the guests to their seats. Escort cards, place cards, and seating charts all work well. The manner in which they are used is as follows:

- **Escort Cards:** Escort cards work in conjunction with place cards to assist guest in finding the correct table and place setting. Escort cards are small note-sized cards with envelopes. The table number is printed on the inside card, with the guest's full name printed on the envelope. These cards are situated alphabetically on a table at or near the entrance to the reception facility. On finding their card, guests will continue to the correct table. Once at the table, place cards, with the guest's full name, will designate exactly which seat the guest will take. This is a traditional formal manner for determining seating.

- **Place Cards:** Place cards, as previously mentioned, are often used with Escort Cards, but they may also be used alone. Place cards are small, tented cards. A display table should be set up at or near the entrance of the reception facility. The place cards should be set up alphabetically. The guest's name and table number are printed on the front of the card. If you wish, the table number may be written inside or on the back of the card. You may choose whether or not to distinguish a particular place setting at the table. Most often with this method, guests select their own seats at the assigned table.

- **Seating Charts:** Seating charts are lists designating the guests' tables. These lists are arranged alphabetically and placed at or near the front entrance of the reception facility. The lists may be placed in a decorative frame for the guests to see, or have a greeter look up the guests' names for them. If the wedding is large, you may want to have two or three frames, so that the guests are not all clamoring to see the one list. Once guests have found their name, they will proceed to the appropriate table. If you wish to distinguish a particular place setting, use a place card at the table.

BEAUTY DO'S AND DON'TS

Every bride wants to look and feel her best on her wedding day. Unfortunately, many brides miss the mark because they have overlooked some very serious do's and don'ts pertaining to wedding day beauty. Avoid these pitfalls by planning and scheduling your beauty routine starting two weeks before the "big day."

Here are some guidelines to follow before you start making appointments.

- Facials should be done one and a half to two weeks before your wedding to avoid unwanted breakouts or redness. Do not schedule a facial during the week prior to the wedding.
- If you are going to visit a day spa (highly recommended for a little prewedding pampering) make the appointment for at least one week prior to the wedding.
- Schedule any facial waxing appointments at least three to five days before the wedding date to prevent the occurrence of unwanted redness or irritation. Do not wax this close to the wedding date if it is your first time.
- If you haven't already done so, have a trial hair and makeup session. If you are having an outdoor wedding, check the makeup in natural light

to ensure you are pleased with the look. When you select a hair and makeup style, you should not look too made up. Rather, you should be a more glamorous version of yourself. Your hair and makeup should complement your dress and your personality, not overwhelm it. Stay away from trendy looks. In a few short years the photos will look dated. A classic look never goes out of style.

- Schedule a haircut. If you regularly color your hair, have it touched up too. Do not try something new or drastic now.
- If you do not get massages on a regular basis, do not schedule one too close to the wedding date. If you are not used to the massage and schedule one in the few days before the wedding, your muscles may be sore.
- Prepare a "Wedding Day Tool Kit" for last-minute beauty emergencies (see page 212).
- Schedule a manicure and/or pedicure for the day before the wedding.
- Don't pick at any pimples or blemishes. Let your makeup artist conceal them for you. In some cases, ice may reduce the swelling.
- Tweeze stray eyebrows (if necessary) the day before.

Here are some final thoughts for you to consider as the wedding day approaches:

- Avoid spending too much time in the sun. Sunburns, tan lines, and peeling are not attractive.
- It is of the utmost importance to remain healthy. Skipping meals to lose that last five pounds is not a wise decision. First of all, your dress will not fit properly, and second, you are going to need the nutrients that are part of a well-balanced meal to keep your energy level up.
- Don't forget to get enough sleep and continue your regular exercise routine.
- Finally, drink plenty of water to keep your skin hydrated and looking fresh.

THE WEDDING PARTY CHECKLIST

Hey everyone! In all the excitement we wouldn't want you to forget anything you will need on the wedding day. Please use the following checklist when you are packing. See you at the rehearsal.

THE GROOMSMEN

☐ Black Dress Socks
☐ Bow Tie
☐ Button Covers
☐ Cologne
☐ Cuff Links
☐ Cummerbund or Vest
☐ Deodorant
☐ Shoes
☐ Toiletries
☐ Tuxedo
☐ Tuxedo Shirt
☐ White Undershirt
☐ Other: _____
☐ Other: _____

THE BRIDESMAIDS

☐ Button Front Shirt (to wear for hair styling and makeup application, so you won't disturb your hair or makeup when changing into your dress)
☐ Deodorant
☐ Dress
☐ Hair Accessories
☐ Hosiery (2 pairs)
☐ Jewelry
☐ Makeup
☐ Perfume
☐ Proper Lingerie
☐ Shoes
☐ Toiletries
☐ Other: _____
☐ Other: _____

THE WEDDING DAY TOOL KIT CHECKLIST

☐ Aspirin or Ibuprofen
☐ Baby or Talcum Powder
☐ Bobby Pins (in white for the bridal veil, and metal)
☐ Bottle of White-Out (last resort for stain cover up on wedding dress)
☐ Bottled Water
☐ Breath Mints
☐ Cellophane Tape (to attach loose cards to the gifts)
☐ Clean Sheet (For the bride to dress on. If the floor surface is tile, linoleum, or wood, the static electricity between the dress and the floor may cause the gown to become dirty while dressing.)
☐ Clean White Cloth (for dabbing off stains on wedding dress)
☐ Clear Band-Aids
☐ Clear Nail Polish (in case someone gets a run in her stockings)
☐ Corsage Pins (extras for boutonnieres and corsages)
☐ Crackers (for nausea and snacks)
☐ Deodorant
☐ Extra Earring Backs
☐ Extra Stockings
☐ Eye Pads or Cream (for puffy eyes)
☐ Facial Tissue or Handkerchief
☐ Hair Spray
☐ Hot Glue Gun (for broken heels, last-minute fixes to decorations, etc.)
☐ Hot Glue Sticks
☐ Money
☐ Mouthwash
☐ Nail Glue
☐ Nail Polish (to match your shade for a quick touch-up)
☐ Rubber Bands
☐ Sanitary Napkins/Tampons
☐ Scissors

☐ Sewing Kit (including straight pins, needle, and thread. Bring white and black thread. Don't forget a color to match the bridesmaid's dresses and the groomsmen's accessories.)

☐ Smelling Salts

☐ Spot Remover

☐ Static Cling Spray

☐ Toothbrush and Toothpaste

☐ Tweezers

☐ White Chalk (for concealing dirt smudges)

☐ Other: _____

☐ Other: _____

☐ Other: _____

☐ Other: _____

8

The Big Day

Congratulations! It is finally here—the day you've been waiting and planning for. Your weeks and months of preparation are all about to come together in the fabulous celebration that is your wedding.

There are just a few more words of wisdom to pass along before it's too late. You want your wedding to come off without a hitch and so do we. You deserve to enjoy this special day. The checklists and final tips in this chapter will aid you in doing just that.

HANDLING LAST-MINUTE ISSUES

You have planned. You have prepared. No detail has been overlooked. Yet no plan is foolproof. As you have undoubtedly experienced in life, you cannot control everyone or everything. It is always possible for plans to go awry. Chances are, if and when something does go wrong, only a handful of people will ever know. At that point, make the best of the situation—"The show must go on."

What follows is a partial list of potential wedding day mishaps and how to deal with them:

Attire Difficulties

Zippers stick, stains appear, things just seem to happen. It can all be fixed, or at least covered up. The items in your Wedding Day Tool Kit (see page 212) should provide you with the tools to solve most of these dilemmas.

Avoid any potential dress disasters by abiding by the following "rules."

1. Do not eat or drink near the dress.
2. When refreshing your makeup, hold a towel over the front and shoulders of the dress.
3. Bring a clean sheet for you to stand on while dressing. Static electricity may cause dirt from a wood, tile, or linoleum floor to cling to the wedding dress.
4. If the gown does get dirty, dab the area gently with a clean white cloth. Do not rub.

The Rings

This is a cause of distress for many brides and grooms. The first problem is the ring not sliding on smoothly during the ceremony. Slide the ring on as far as it will go and have the bride or groom discreetly finish putting it on.

If someone forgets the ring/rings—fake it. You can always borrow a ring from a family member if you need the prop. If time and distance permit, have a friend or family member pick the ring up before the reception.

If you will be wearing gloves, open the seams on either side of the ring finger, so that you may easily slip your finger out during the ceremony.

Finally, avoid this last ring disaster before it happens—do not let the ring bearer have the real rings; leave that job to the honor attendants. Tie fake rings onto the ring pillow.

Weather

You cannot control nature. Make provisions if you are marrying during unpredictable weather. If the ceremony is being held outdoors, have a contingency plan. As a backup, place a tent on hold, or if there is a banquet hall or ballroom on the premises, talk to the site coordinator about reserving that room in case of inclement weather.

Absentees

You may have a flaky or flu-stricken bridesmaid or groomsman in your midst. Should this happen, it is easy to cover up. Just ignore it (for now anyway). Rearranging the processional and recessional is an easy matter to tackle. The number of bridesmaids and groomsmen does not have to be equal anyway.

Fainting

If you are aware that a family member or someone in the wedding party is prone to fainting, prepare ahead of time. Have one of your attendants carry some smelling salts down the aisle with them in case of emergency. If it is an extremely hot day, or the ceremony is lengthy, make provision ahead of time. Leave the front row or pew open for the wedding party to be seated during the ceremony.

Instruct everyone that if something should happen, the person should be discreetly helped to a seat in the front, and not to make an issue of it. The ceremony should continue, unless of course it's you or the groom. Then you should take the time you need to regain your composure.

Health Problems

Should you or the groom become ill, as long as it is not too serious, the best that can be done is to go on with the wedding as scheduled. Call your doctor and see if there is anything that she can do. Take it easy and get as much rest as you can. Makeup can do wonders, and most of the guests will never know. Please refer to the FAQ section in the Appendix for information relating to more serious health issues.

Vendor No-Shows

It is rare that a reputable wedding professional with whom you have signed a contract and confirmed the details will not show up, or fail to provide the designated product. When you hire a reputable vendor she knows the in's and out's of the business, and takes her job seriously. She will do whatever needs to be done to arrive at your wedding as scheduled.

However, every once in a while obstacles get in the way. For example, someone falls ill, or gets into a traffic accident, and is unable to perform duties or services as planned. If something like this should occur, the first step is to talk with your other wedding vendors. In a situation like this, most vendors will be happy to help you out. Their connections and knowledge of the wedding business can be a great benefit, as they can refer you to other vendors.

If the referrals the other vendors provide you with are booked, you still have other invaluable resources at your disposal. Go through the pages of your regional bridal magazine and start calling the vendors listed in these sources, looking for someone who is available on your wedding day. Ask your friends, family, or wedding party to help you make the phone calls. There are many wedding professionals in each and every category, and it is unlikely they will all be booked on that particular day.

This may not be the ideal circumstance for hiring a wedding professional, but drastic circumstances call for quick thinking and action. You will most likely not have the time to thoroughly interview the vendor, nor will you be able to pick and choose. If it means the difference between having or not having photographs of your wedding or carrying a bouquet down the aisle, you will make it work.

WEDDING DAY NERVES

Not often will you find a bride or groom who isn't having a case of the nerves. Wedding day nerves are often due to worries over the outcome of the wedding. Will everything fall into place? Will the flower girl make it down the aisle? Even the most pulled together bride is bound to experience a little wedding day anxiety.

Learning to put the day and the event in perspective is important. Even if the cake topples over, the most important event has occurred; you have married the one you love. Remember that each and every person has a different vision of perfection. There is no way you can or will please all people on your wedding day. Most important is to please yourself and your fiancé.

The following are a few ways to relieve anxiety, de-stress, or just plain relax before you walk down the aisle.

- Eat. Brides tend not to eat, which makes them edgy and tired. A small snack before the ceremony will alleviate this problem. Try to avoid greasy or heavy foods. Ask the caterer to bring some hors d'oeuvres to the wedding party after the ceremony. Don't forget to ask the caterer to pack a snack (using the leftovers) for you and the groom to take to your hotel room after the wedding reception.
- Surround yourself with pleasant and helpful people. Avoid "toxic" people before the wedding.
- While waiting for the ceremony to begin, find a room as far away from the commotion as possible. The footsteps of the guests arriving and the final details being put into place are bound to cause tension and anxiety.
- Try to think positively. Daydream if necessary. Transport yourself to another place. Think about the wonderful honeymoon that is to come.
- Find some time for yourself. Take a bath, read, or exercise the night before or early that morning.
- Do something that does not involve the wedding for at least fifteen minutes.
- Come to the realization that you have done all you can do.
- If you are religious, pray.
- Remember what the day is *really* for—marrying the one you love.
- Delegate duties. Let your family, friends, and wedding party help. That is why they are there.
- Designate a "Troubleshooter" so you will not be bothered with small problems or issues.
- Spend some time with your fiancé. If seeing or talking to him will alleviate some stress and reassure you everything will be OK, do it—even if it is before the ceremony.

TO TIP OR NOT TO TIP

A tip is presented to someone as an expression of gratitude for gracious and efficient service. A vendor should not expect a tip, as you have already paid him a fee to perform a specific duty. If you are exceptionally pleased with his work, attitude, and/or performance, then a tip may be in order.

When you are dealing with wedding vendors, you must be aware that some vendors, like the caterer and reception facility, may have already included a service fee in their bill. This service fee is their tip. Refer to your contract to determine if such a charge has been added to your bill.

The last thing you need to do on your wedding day is fish around in your purse for tip money. Take some time the day before the wedding to prepare tip envelopes—write the vendor's name on the outside of the envelope, enclose the appropriate amount, and seal it. Ask someone to be the designated "tipper." Have this person wait until the end of the evening before handing out the tips.

Tips for Tipping

The following are some basic guidelines for tipping. Upscale establishments and larger cities often call for larger tips.

- **Caterer/Site Coordinator/Manager:** Refer to your contract to determine if you have already been charged a service fee. Even if this fee has been added, if you were exceptionally pleased with her work, you may wish to present her with a small gift or additional tip. If the service fee is not included in the bill, a tip of 15 to 20 percent of the bill is customary.
- **Service Personnel:** Refer to your contract to determine if you have already been charged a service fee. If not, decide upon a dollar amount (like $20), and multiply that by the number of service personnel. These tips are usually paid to the site coordinator or banquet manager, who will disperse the individual tips later.
- **Bartender:** Refer to your contract to determine if you have already been charged a service fee. If the fee is not included in the bill, 10 percent of the liquor bill is appropriate.

- **Parking Attendants/Coat Room/Powder Room Attendant:** Refer to your contract to determine if you have already been charged a service fee. If not, $.50 to $1 per guest or car is acceptable. If you do not want your guests to feel obligated to tip, make arrangements with the management to have a gratuity paid in a lump sum, by the host (you), at the end of the evening.
- **Limousine Driver:** Refer to your contract to determine if you have already been charged a service fee. Otherwise 15 to 20 percent of the bill is customary.
- **Musicians/Disc Jockey:** Not usually included in the bill, tipping the musicians or DJ is entirely optional. If you choose to do so, $20 to $25 per person is appropriate.
- **Other Vendors:** Not usually included in the bill. If you wish to tip them, 10 to 20 percent of the bill is acceptable.
- **Delivery Personnel:** Deliveries are usually considered to be part of the service, and there may already be a fee for deliveries in your contract. Tipping the delivery personnel is optional. If you choose to do so, $5 to $10 a person is appropriate.
- **Consultant:** Choosing to tip your consultant is optional. If you choose to do so, after the wedding, present your consultant with a thank-you note for her service, and include a tip with it.

CHECKLISTS
OF WHAT TO BRING

You have planned and prepared. Now that the wedding day is finally here, you don't want to leave anything behind. Use the checklists at the end of this chapter for yourself and the groom to remind you of what items you will need to bring with you on the wedding day. There is also a checklist for wedding accessories and decorations. Checklists for the wedding party can be found on page 211. You can modify these checklists to fit your specific needs by blacking out or adding items.

THE GROOM'S CHECKLIST

- ☐ Black Dress Socks
- ☐ Bow Tie
- ☐ Button Covers
- ☐ Cash for Tipping
- ☐ Cellular Phone
- ☐ Checkbook
- ☐ Cologne
- ☐ Contact Lenses and Saline Solution
- ☐ Credit Cards
- ☐ Cuff Links
- ☐ Cummerbund
- ☐ Deodorant
- ☐ Getaway Clothes
- ☐ Gift for Bride
- ☐ Glasses
- ☐ Handkerchief
- ☐ Honeymoon Luggage
- ☐ Marriage License
- ☐ Pager
- ☐ Shoes
- ☐ Suspenders
- ☐ Toiletries
- ☐ Tuxedo
- ☐ Tuxedo Shirt
- ☐ Underwear
- ☐ Vest
- ☐ Wedding Night Bag
- ☐ Wedding Ring(s)
- ☐ Wedding Vows
- ☐ White Undershirt
- ☐ Other: _____
- ☐ Other: _____
- ☐ Other: _____

THE BRIDE'S CHECKLIST

☐ Blow Dryer
☐ Button Front Shirt (to wear for hair styling and makeup application, so you won't disturb your hair or makeup when changing into your wedding dress.)
☐ Cellular Phone
☐ Ceremony Shoes
☐ Contact Lenses and Saline Solution
☐ Corset or Proper Lingerie
☐ Curling Iron
☐ Deodorant
☐ Dress Bag
☐ Extra Itineraries
☐ Getaway Clothes
☐ Gift for Groom
☐ Glasses
☐ Gloves
☐ Handkerchief
☐ Honeymoon Luggage
☐ Hosiery (2 pairs)
☐ Hot Rollers
☐ Iron or Steamer
☐ Jewelry
☐ Keepsake Garter
☐ Makeup
☐ Pager
☐ Perfume
☐ Portable Planner (see Chapter One)
☐ Reception Shoes
☐ Slip or Crinoline
☐ Something Old, Something New, Something Borrowed, Something Blue
☐ Throwaway Garter

- ☐ Toiletries
- ☐ Veil and/or Headpiece
- ☐ Wedding Day Tool Kit (see page 212)
- ☐ Wedding Dress
- ☐ Wedding Night Bag
- ☐ Wedding Vows
- ☐ Other: _____
- ☐ Other: _____

WEDDING ACCESSORIES CHECKLIST

- ☐ Aisle Runner
- ☐ Bubbles, Birdseed, or Rose Petals (for tossing)
- ☐ Cake Knife and Server
- ☐ Cake Topper
- ☐ Card Box (for gift table)
- ☐ Centerpieces
- ☐ Decorations
- ☐ Disposable Table Cameras
- ☐ Engagement Photos
- ☐ Favors
- ☐ Flower Girl Basket
- ☐ Guest Book
- ☐ Pens for Guest Book
- ☐ Place Cards
- ☐ Ring Pillow
- ☐ Table Numbers
- ☐ Toasting Goblets
- ☐ Unity Candle
- ☐ Wedding Programs
- ☐ Other: _____
- ☐ Other: _____

☐ Other: _____

☐ Other: _____

NOTE

There may be additional items pertaining to particular customs and religions. Add them to the end of this list.

ADDITIONAL COMMENTS:

_____

_____

_____

_____

_____

_____

_____

_____

_____

_____

_____

_____

_____

_____

_____

_____

_____

_____

_____

_____

9

The Honeymoon

Aaaah!!! It's relaxing just thinking about it. After the hustle and bustle of your wedding day, the honeymoon will be the perfect antidote for you and your new husband. This trip will likely be one of the most romantic journeys you will ever have the pleasure of experiencing. Take some time to get prepared, and know that it will all help to ensure that the trip of your dreams becomes a reality. If wrapping up the details for your impending wedding has left you too strapped for time, know that many of the honeymoon preparations mentioned below can be delegated to your fiancé, willing family members, or friends.

REALLY KNOW WHERE YOU'RE GOING

Though you may have already done plenty of research about your honeymoon destination prior to booking the trip, take the initiative to learn more about what's happening there right now. Speak to someone at the board of tourism, or ask to speak to the concierge at the hotel where you will be staying. Do some research on the Internet, or look for any recent news coverage on the region. These steps will help to protect you and your fiancé from any unwanted surprises upon your arrival. Try to find out the following information about the destination that you will soon be visiting:

- Current weather conditions
- If there has been any recent damage in the area caused by natural disasters
- Is there anything going on regionally or politically that will affect your safety or comfort while visiting?
- Will there be any special events going on, such as festivals, conventions, fairs, or traveling exhibits during your stay?
- Is there any scheduled road or airport construction that will impede your ability to get to your destination?
- Is there any scheduled construction at your resort, hotel, or inn? If so, ask to be placed in a room as far away from the construction as possible.
- Are there any required or recommended immunizations that need to be administered before arrival?
- Are current passports and visas required?
- Will your credit card company or automobile insurance policy cover insurance on a rental car at your destination?

If your research uncovers anything that concerns you (for example, dangerous weather or political conditions), contact your travel agent right away. Discuss with her what your options are for traveling to an alternate destination. Be sure to thoroughly review the terms of any travel insurance you may have purchased before making any changes.

SHOPPING, SHOPPING, SHOPPING

There may be some last-minute shopping to do before you can fill your suitcases with all of the necessary gear for the type of honeymoon you will be taking. To help you prepare, review the packing lists provided at the end of this chapter for some hints on items you may still need to purchase. Some of the popular items that couples purchase for their honeymoons include:

- Clothing (appropriate for the destination's climate and culture)
- Bathing Suits
- Travel-Size Toiletries
- Luggage, Tags, and Locks
- A Travel Hair Dryer
- Travel Electrical Adapters
- Traveler's Checks and Foreign Currency
- A Camera and Rolls of Film
- A Video Camera and Tapes
- Sporting Gear (snorkel gear, scuba gear, skis, etc.)
- Sexy Lingerie and Items for Romance

LEAVING HOME

If you are taking a long honeymoon trip, there are a few preparations that you may want to make for your home—before you leave. If you do not have a house-sitter lined up, have the post office hold your mail until you return, or ask a neighbor to periodically collect it for you. Confirm arrangements with your pet sitter or kennel. Ask any stores with which you have registered to hold any deliveries of gifts, and also place a hold on any daily newspaper or magazine subscriptions. Don't forget to start emptying out your refrigerator of any perishable items. You won't want to be greeted with a foul smelling kitchen upon your return from paradise.

THE JOURNEY

Taking the steps to ensure a problem-free and comfortable journey to your honeymoon destination is the most important preparation of all. About a week before your departure date, confirm the following details:

- Airline flight numbers and departure times
- Restrictions on luggage
- Special meal requests
- Seat reservations
- Hotel reservations
- Rental car reservations
- Transportation to and from the airport
- That you have possession of all travel documents (see the list of What to Pack for Your Honeymoon—Documents and Paperwork on page 230)
- All luggage is in working order and is accessorized with the proper tags and locks

The day of departure for your big adventure, consider stocking your hand-carried bag with the following items to keep you and your fiancé more comfortable and happy on your trip: bottled water, energizing snacks, moisturizer, travel pillows, reading material, eye shades, ear plugs, or a portable cassette or CD player, and enough cash to cover any expenses or purchases en route.

SPECIAL TOUCHES

About this time, also be thinking of any ways you can make this trip even more special for you and your new spouse. Consider making prior arrangements to set up the following special touches:

- Call the hotel and arrange for a special room service delivery of your favorite champagne, beverages, food, or desserts upon arrival.
- Arrange for a gift basket full of treats, or a beautiful floral arrangement to be waiting in the room for your new bride or groom.
- Have the hotel staff set the scene for romance by filling the room with lighted candles, scattering rose petals on the bed, lighting the fireplace, or perhaps having a warm bubble bath already drawn in which the newlyweds could immediately unwind.
- Make advance reservations through the hotel's concierge for a romantic dinner for your first night.

- Also speak to the concierge about reservations for any popular excursions in the area, such as a helicopter ride through the rain forest, a day sail to a secluded island for lunch, or a horse-drawn sleigh ride through the woods.

As the crowning touch for your romantic vacation, consider upgrading your airline tickets or hotel room upon check-in (assuming you do not already have a full first-class voyage reserved). Use accumulated frequent flier miles, or some of that extra gift money you received from Aunt Eva to purchase last-minute upgrades that are offered, if space is available. Make sure that everyone knows you are on your honeymoon. Don't be shy! Everybody loves honeymooners, and loves to throw lots of free perks their way.

WHAT TO PACK FOR YOUR HONEYMOON CHECKLIST

DOCUMENTS AND PAPERWORK:

HIS   HERS

—   —   -Airline Tickets

—   —   -Passports

—   —   -Visas

—   —   -Driver's Licenses or Photo Identification Cards

—   —   -Cash and/or Foreign Currency

—   —   -Traveler's Checks

—   —   -Credit Cards

—   —   -Vaccination Certificates

—   —   -Car and House Keys

—   —   -Books and Magazines to Read

—   —   -A Complete Travel Itinerary (with contact numbers for travel agent)

—   —   -Hotel Information and Confirmation Numbers

—   —   -Rental Car Information and Confirmation Numbers

—   —   -Guide Books

—   —   -Foreign Language Dictionary

—   —   -Exchange Rate Calculator

TOILETRIES:

HIS   HERS

—   —   -Toothbrush

—   —   -Toothpaste and Other Dental Care Products

—   -Makeup and Other Beauty Care Products

—   —   -Hair Care Products

HIS	HERS	
___	___	-Soap and Skin Care Products
___	___	-Sunscreen
___	___	-Insect Repellent
___	___	-Lotion/Moisturizer
___	___	-Deodorant
___	___	-Eyeglasses
___	___	-Contact Lenses and Saline Solution
___	___	-Razors
___	___	-Shaving Cream and Aftershave
___	___	-Perfume or Cologne
___	___	-Manicure Kit
	___	-Feminine Hygiene Products
___	___	-Birth Control
___	___	-Hair Dryer (with electrical adapter if necessary)

WARM/TROPICAL CLIMATE CLOTHING AND ACCESSORIES:

HIS	HERS	
___	___	-Shorts
___	___	-Shirts
	___	-Sundresses
	___	-Skirts
___	___	-Pants and Jeans
___	___	-Appropriate Dinner Clothing
___	___	-Sleepwear
___	___	-Undergarments
___	___	-Socks

WHAT TO PACK FOR YOUR HONEYMOON CHECKLIST (CONT'D)

HIS   HERS

___   ___   -Bathing Suits

___   ___   -Beach Sandals/Slippers

___   ___   -Beach Bag

___   ___   -Bathing Suit Cover-ups/Sarongs

___   ___   -Beach Towels (if not provided)

___   ___   -Hats

___   ___   -Sunglasses

         ___   -Purse

___   ___   -Waist Pouch or Backpack

___   ___   -Sports Gear

___   ___   -Walking Shoes

___   ___   -Hiking Boots

___   ___   -Umbrellas

___   ___   -Mosquito Netting

___   ___   -Camera and Film

___   ___   -Video Camera and Tapes

COLD CLIMATE CLOTHING AND ACCESSORIES:

HIS   HERS

___   ___   -Pants

___   ___   -Long-Sleeve Shirts

___   ___   -Thermal Underwear

___   ___   -Jeans

___   ___   -Sweaters

HIS	HERS	
___	___	-Turtlenecks
	___	-Warm Dresses
___	___	-Appropriate Dinner Clothing
___	___	-Sleepwear
___	___	-Undergarments
___	___	-Socks
___	___	-Boots
___	___	-Walking Shoes
___	___	-Gloves
___	___	-Warm Hats
___	___	-Coats
	___	-Purse
___	___	-Waist Pouch or Backpack
___	___	-Sports Gear
___	___	-Umbrella
___	___	-Camera and Film
___	___	-Video Camera and Tapes

ITEMS FOR ROMANCE:

HIS	HERS	
___	___	-Sexy Lingerie
___	___	-Robes
___	___	-Massage Oils
___	___	-Scented Candles
___	___	-Bubble Bath

ADDITIONAL COMMENTS:

_____

_____

_____

_____

_____

_____

_____

_____

_____

_____

_____

_____

_____

_____

_____

_____

_____

_____

_____

_____

_____

_____

_____

_____

_____

10

Wrapping Things Up

After months of planning, picking out dresses, and meeting with vendors, it is finally time to relax and enjoy your new journey—married life. But before you get too comfortable, there are a few more details that must be attended to.

WEDDING ANNOUNCEMENTS

(Before the Honeymoon)

Wedding announcements are sent to distant relatives and friends who were not invited to the wedding. Announcements should not be sent to those who attended or were invited to the ceremony and/or reception. There is no obligation to send wedding announcements. They are, however, particularly useful if you have a small wedding, were married far from home, or have an unusually large family, many of whom were not invited to the wedding.

Should you decide to send announcements, have them printed at the same time your invitations are printed. The announcements should be similar in style to the original invitation. They should state the wedding has taken place and include the following information: name of parents or host (if applicable), name of bride and groom, date, and place of marriage. Prepare and address the announcements at the same time that you are preparing your wedding invitations. Be sure to keep the announcements separate, as they should be mailed the day of or the day after the wedding ceremony—not before.

Sample wording for a wedding announcement:

Kathy Marie Smith

and

Steven Matthew Monroe

announce their marriage

Saturday, the first of July

Two thousand

Hollywood, California

You may also want to announce your marriage in the local newspaper. Wedding announcements are usually published within a month or two of the wedding date. The guidelines for each publication vary. Some require a fee to publish the announcement, and others are free of charge. Most publications will print a photo along with the announcement as well. Call each publication to obtain a copy of its guidelines, restrictions, and fees.

PRESERVE THE MEMORIES

(Before the Honeymoon)

While your photographs will capture the magic of your wedding day for years to come, preserving some more tangible items from your wedding is something you may wish to consider. Preserving your gown or your bridal bouquet are a couple of the most pressing matters in this case.

The Bridal Bouquet

If you wish to preserve your bridal bouquet, arrangements will need to be made at least one month ahead of time. Preserving your bridal bouquet involves more than pressing or drying the flowers. Rather, it is a process that utilizes freeze-drying or other special chemicals to preserve the flowers as they were on your wedding day. You might want to consider having the groom's boutonniere preserved as well.

Once you have chosen a company to preserve your bouquet, the company will ship you a special box for transporting it, as well as special instructions for handling the bouquet. The day of or after the wedding, your bouquet will need to be shipped back to the company for them to finish the preservation process. Be sure to follow the specific instructions the company supplies.

You can find companies for bridal bouquet preservation at bridal shows, in regional and national magazines, through a wedding consultant, or a wedding planning and resource center. Preserving your bridal bouquet is not inexpensive. Prices start at $150 and go up from there. If this is too expensive for your budget, consider drying or pressing the flowers yourself. A visit to your local library, bookstore, or craft store should provide you with the information and instructions to do this on your own.

The Wedding Gown

For most women, their wedding gown is the most exquisite and expensive garment they will ever own or wear. However, once you have worn your wedding gown, there will probably be little need for it, until one day when maybe your daughter will choose to wear it. While some brides re-sell their dress and some put it in the back of their closets, having your dress professionally preserved is the only way to ensure its beauty for years to come.

Arrangements should be made for preserving your gown prior to the wedding day, as the gown should be taken in soon after the wedding. Consult with the company or dry cleaner you have selected for a recommendation on how long to wait before bringing in the gown. Depending on their recommendation, you may want to ask your mother or a close friend to take the gown in while you are on your honeymoon.

Even if there are no visible stains on the gown, you may want to wait a week or two before cleaning and preserving it. Some stains, such as perspiration, take longer to surface than others. It is important to let these stains appear so that you know which areas of the gown need to be cleaned more thoroughly. If you do wait a week or two, do not leave your gown hanging. This may cause the fabric to stretch and sag. And finally, do not cover the gown in a plastic bag, as this may cause yellowing.

In the preservation process your gown will be treated with a special chemical process to prevent the deterioration and discoloration of the fabric. The wedding dress will then be placed in a box and vacuum sealed. Many of these boxes come with a special window so you may view your gown. The window and all packaging materials should be acid free.

Some companies do not use a window, but rather package the dress in a sealed box. Make sure the dry cleaner or company you entrust with this precious garment is reputable. Take precautions and do your homework. Keep in mind once the box is sealed, you will not be able to see your dress without spoiling the seal. You must feel confident in the company's ability, honesty, and ethics in this case.

Many dry cleaning establishments preserve wedding gowns. There are also a number of specialized companies that perform this service. If you decide to have your gown preserved, use the same caution you have used throughout your wedding planning—ask questions and get the facts in writing.

Preserving your bridal gown can be costly. Prices start at about $100 and go up from there. Talk to friends who have had their gowns preserved to obtain recommendations for this service. You can also find information on gown preservation or dry cleaners that perform this service in bridal magazines and the yellow pages. Don't forget to check the Internet for additional information.

Before you hand over your gown, talk with an expert at that location and find out how much the preservation will actually cost. Most importantly, do not sign a waiver/release/disclaimer releasing the company of responsibility while the gown is in its care.

THANK-YOU'S

(After the Honeymoon)

Most brides dread the task of writing thank-you notes, not because they are ungrateful but because it is a time-consuming project. This is especially true if they had a large wedding. However, this task should never go undone. A written thank-you is called for even if you have expressed your gratitude verbally.

One of the most important rules in writing thank-you cards is that the note be handwritten. Computer generated or preprinted notes are no-no's. If you should decide to order thank-you notes that include a preprinted message, you should always add a personal note. Other than that, writing the thank-you cards is relatively simple. They need not be long, but they should include the following:

- A mention of the gift. For monetary gifts, you do not mention the money or include the amount, but rather refer to it as the "generous gift," or something similar.
- A sentence about how you intend to use the gift or how lovely it will look in your new home.
- A personal statement or comment about how much you enjoyed that person's presence at the wedding, or thank them for attending.

Sample Thank-You Note (sent after the wedding)

> Dear Aunt Sally and Uncle Bob,
>
> Thank you so much for the lovely crystal vase. It will make a beautiful centerpiece in our dining room. Every time we see it, we will remember our beautiful wedding, as well as your warm wishes for our new life together. We are so glad you were there to share our special day.
> Love,
> Bride and Groom

For any gifts you receive prior to the wedding, thank-you cards should be sent within two to three weeks. For gifts received at or after the wedding, attempt to get the thank-you's on the way as soon as possible after returning from the honeymoon. When writing thank-you notes, sooner is better; however, the accepted rule is within three months of the wedding date. Keep in mind, this may be a continuing process. Etiquette dictates that guests have one year from the wedding date to send gifts.

There may be a few people who deserve a little something special for the love and support they have provided throughout this whole process. Acknowledge these important people with a nice gift. Consider sending flowers to your families the day after the wedding, or presenting your "Troubleshooter" with a gift certificate for a day spa or nice restaurant. If your wedding party has been extremely helpful you may want to extend an extra thank-you by hosting a casual lunch or dinner for them once you return from the honeymoon and are settled into married life.

THE NAME GAME

(After the Honeymoon)

A frequent question for brides today is "Will you change your name?" When it comes to making this decision there are a number of options. The decision of whether or not to change or alter your name is a personal decision between you and your husband. You will have to consider the pros and cons of each option before you make a final decision.

The options for your name include:

- The traditional—drop your maiden name and adopt your husband's name.
- Keep your maiden name.
- Keep your maiden name for business only and take your husband's name for all other (social) purposes.
- Hyphenate your name. In this instance, only the woman may hyphenate, or her husband may choose to hyphenate his name as well.
- Adopt your maiden name as a middle name and use your husband's name as your last name.
- Have your husband take your last name.
- While less common, some couples combine their names and invent a new surname.

There are many issues involved when it comes to making this decision. What is important is that you do what is right for you and your husband. Spreading the news about your decision can be done in a variety of ways.

- When ordering thank-you or informal cards, have the full names you and your husband will be known by printed on them. For example:
    > Mr. and Mrs. John Smith
    > or
    > Ms. Kathy Jones and
    > Mr. John Smith
- Include at-home cards with the announcements, invitations, or thank-you cards. Have the appropriate names and/or titles printed on them (see above example).
- For business purposes, if you will be changing or altering your name, you may wish to have a name card or other formal announcement printed with your new name. These should be mailed to business associates.
- Include the appropriate names and titles in any marriage announcements published in the newspaper or other publication. You may wish to state "Ms. Kathy Jones will retain her maiden name," or something similar.
- Have yourselves announced by the appropriate names as your enter the reception. Or, if you don't want to make a distinction at that time, have yourselves announced by your first names only.

Whatever option you choose, it is important to remain consistent for legal purposes. If you will be changing or altering your name in any way, you will need to follow up with the proper legal paperwork. Some of the items or people that you will need to update are:

- Accountant
- Bank Accounts
- Car Title and Registration
- Credit Cards
- Deeds to Property
- Driver's License
- Employer and/or School Records
- Health Care Providers

- Insurance Documents (car, life, health, homeowners, etc.)
- Lawyer
- Loans (car, student loans, etc.)
- Magazine, Newspaper, and Professional Subscriptions
- Memberships (health club, video stores, library, frequent flier miles)
- Mortgage
- P.O. Box
- Passport
- Professional Associations
- Retirement Account
- Social Security
- Stock or Investment Accounts
- Tax Information
- Utility Companies
- Voter Registration (some states do this automatically when you change your driver's license)
- Will

Call the appropriate offices to obtain the information you will need to change these documents. Some agencies require you to come in to their offices. Others will send you forms in the mail, and with others, you may be able to obtain any necessary forms over the Internet and fill them out before you visit the office.

Ask each agency if there is any additional paperwork or information you need to bring with you to your appointment. Many agencies require official proof of the marriage, such as a certified marriage license with the state seal. Photocopies are often unacceptable.

If this seems like a lot to undertake, you may consider purchasing a name change kit, such as The Official New Bride Name Change Kit (1-800-439-0334). You can find information on this kit and others in national and regional bridal magazines and on the Internet. They cost approximately $20, and provide a step-by-step guide for changing your name, including many of the forms you will need to do so.

THE WEDDING GOWN PRESERVATION

Name of Company: _____

Contact's Name: _____

Phone: _____

Fax: _____

E-mail: _____

Address: _____

QUESTIONS TO ASK

- How soon should I send the gown to you?

- Do you clean the gown first? Is there an additional charge?

- Will you perform minor repairs?

- May I include shoes, veil, garter, gloves, or other accessories in the package with the dress?

- How do you perform the preservation process?

- Do you use acid-free materials to package and store the gown?

- Do you offer delivery and pickup? Is it included in your charges?

- Do you offer a warranty covering the replacement value of the gown, should something go wrong while in your possession or in the preservation process?

- Do you have professionals trained in textile preservation overseeing the process?

THE WEDDING GOWN PRESERVATION (CONT'D)

- When can I expect the process to be completed and the gown delivered to me?

- (If there is no window on the packaging) How can I be sure the gown I get back is mine?

ADDITIONAL COMMENTS:

_____

_____

_____

_____

_____

_____

_____

_____

_____

_____

_____

_____

_____

_____

_____

_____

_____

_____

Appendix
Wedding Info at a Glance

BRIDAL PUBLICATIONS

National Magazines

Bridal Guide	800-834-9998
Bride's Magazine	800-456-6162
Elegant Bride	336-378-6065
For the Bride by Demetrios	212-967-0750
Martha Stewart Living Weddings	800-999-6518
Modern Bride	800-777-5786

Special Interests Magazines
(Available nationwide)

Bridal Crafts	800-444-0441
Latina Bride	626-296-1249
Signature Bride: Bridal Lifestyles for Today's Black Bride	312-335-8774
Sposa	416-364-5899

Special Editions
(Available nationwide)

InStyle Magazine	800-274-6200
People Magazine	800-541-9000
Town and Country	800-289-8696

Regional Magazines Publishers

(Call for specific information for your region.)

Modern Bride Connection	800-848-6664
Wedding Bells	800-387-9877
The Wedding Pages	800-843-4983

INTERNET ADDRESSES

www.howtoidoweddings.com

www.bridal-show.com

www.brides.com

www.ElegantBrideMagazine.com

www.iBride.com

www.modernbride.com

www.planningpotpourri.com

www.theknot.com

www.usabride.com

www.waycoolweddings.com

www.weddingbells.com

www.weddingchannel.com

www.weddingcircle.com

www.weddinghelpers.com

www.weddingorders.com

www.weddingpages.com

www.wedding411.com

www.wednet.com

www.wedserv.com

FREQUENTLY ASKED QUESTIONS (FAQ)

Attire

I have one bridesmaid who is a large size, while my others are petite. What can I do about finding a dress that flatters all of them?

All of the dresses do not need to be the same style. If you choose to go this route, all of the dresses should be the same color (and possibly the same fabric). The hem lengths should also be the same. Another option is to have the dress custom-made. Another is to order from a company that carries large sizes as well as regular sizes. In this instance, you may be able to find flattering dresses in the same fabric and color without the cost of custom-made dresses. And, finally, you can let each bridesmaid choose her own dress. Give all of them guidelines on style, color, and hem lengths. The fabric will not be the same.

Which way do the pleats go on the cummerbund?

The pleats face up. Think of it as a crumb catcher.

Bridal Showers

I am having a small wedding with only family. My Maid of Honor (my sister) would like to host a bridal shower for other friends. Is it rude to invite friends to the bridal shower who are not invited to the wedding?

This is acceptable as long as the Maid of Honor explains the circumstances.

May I include "Registered at . . ." cards with the bridal shower invitations?

It is acceptable to include these cards with the bridal shower invitations.

Ceremony

What do I do with my engagement ring during the ceremony?

Wear your engagement ring on your right hand, or have the Maid of Honor hold it for you until after the ceremony, and then slip it on, placed on top of your wedding band. The wedding ring should go on first, and be worn closest to your heart.

I have an uneven number of bridesmaids and groomsmen. How should they walk for the processional and recessional?

You may want to consider having the groomsmen already in their ceremony positions, and the bridesmaids walk the processional alone. During the recessional, the wedding party can file out one by one, boy-girl, boy-girl, or each groomsmen can escort two bridesmaids, or vice versa.

Neither of us belong to a church. Where do we find an officiant?

Regional bridal magazines have many ads for officiants who will perform a ceremony for you. Some areas even have a toll-free number to call for referrals.

Flowers

How can I distinguish my Maid of Honor from the other bridesmaids?

The Maid of Honor can wear a floral wreath on her head, or have a slightly different bouquet from the other bridesmaids; for instance, she may have flowing ribbons, or a special color of ribbon. Her dress style may differ as well.

I have many bridesmaids and a small budget. Those bouquets can be pretty expensive. What can I do to cut costs?

Have each bridesmaid carry a single flower, perhaps a rose. Tie a bow with some beautiful ribbon, and have each of them carry this down the aisle. You may want to have the Maid of Honor carry a bouquet to distinguish her.

Floral centerpieces are so expensive. What is another option?

Use potted or flowering plants as centerpieces. The plants are inexpensive, and you can paint the pot to match the colors of your wedding. These centerpieces are easy to put together. They make a great alternative to expensive floral arrangements, and guests get to take home a living keepsake from your wedding.

Invitations

How do I address the envelopes . . .

First of all, the outer envelope should include the full names of the invitees—first, last, and the proper titles (Mr. and Mrs. John Henry Smith). The inner envelope should include the proper titles and last names only (Mr. and Mrs. Smith). For children under eighteen, list only their first names, under their parents' names, on the inner envelope in birth order.

for a married couple with different last names?

List the names on separate lines alphabetically

(Outer Envelope) Ms. Kathy Jones   (Inner) Ms. Jones and Mr. Smith
                 Mr. John Smith
                 1818 Wedding Bell Drive
                 I Do, California 90273

for an unmarried couple living together?

You may send them one invitation. Each person's full name should be on a separate line, with the address following. List the names alphabetically (see sample):

(Outer Envelope) Ms. Kathy Jones   (Inner) Ms. Jones and Mr. Smith
                 Mr. John Smith
                 1818 Wedding Bell Drive
                 I Do, California 90273

if the wife is a doctor or has a special title?

The names should be on separate lines with the wife's full title and name. The wife's name is listed first (see sample):

(Outer Envelope) Dr. Kathy Smith   (Inner) Dr. Smith and Mr. Smith
                 Mr. John Smith
                 1818 Wedding Bell Drive
                 I Do, California 90273

if the man is a doctor or has a special title?

(Outer Envelope) Dr. and Mrs. John Smith   (Inner) Dr. and Mrs. Smith
1818 Wedding Bell Drive
I Do, California 90273

if the husband and wife are both doctors?

(Outer Envelope) The Doctors Smith   (Inner) The Doctors Smith
1818 Wedding Bell Drive
I Do, California 90273

if the guest is in the military?

Spell out the person's name and include the branch of service. Include the guest's rank if above sergeant. If the guest's rank is below that of sergeant, use his/her name (without a title) and the branch of service.

(Outer Envelope) Captain John Smith   (Inner) Captain Smith
United States Army
1818 Wedding Bell Drive
I Do, California 90273

OR

(Outer Envelope) John Smith   (Inner) Mr. Smith
United States Army
1818 Wedding Bell Drive
I Do, California 90273

for an entire family?

The parents' names are used on the outer envelope. The children's names (those under eighteen) are listed on the inner envelope under the parents names, according to their birth order. Try to avoid using "and Family."

(Outer Envelope) Mr. and Mrs. John Smith (Inner)
1818 Wedding Bell Drive   Mr. and Mrs. Smith
I Do, California 90273   Jennifer, Robert, and Ann

if children over the age of eighteen are living at home?

They are issued their own invitation.

(Outer Envelope) Ms. Jennifer Jones   (Inner) Ms. Jones
1818 Wedding Bell Drive
I Do, California 90273

for the boyfriend/girlfriend of an invited guest who do not live together?

A boyfriend or girlfriend of an invited guest should receive his/her own invitation. Try not to use the phrase "and Guest" on the inner or outer envelope.

How do I assemble the invitations?

Begin with the invitation. Place the tissue paper on the invitation (printed side up). Place any additional inserts on top of the invitation and tissue, according to size, from largest to smallest, printed side up. Place this stack into the ungummed inner envelope, with the text facing the flap. The guests' names should have already been printed on the inner envelope. Then place this whole ensemble into the large lined outer envelope, with the guests' names facing the back flap. Be sure to address the envelopes before stuffing them.

Can I send one invitation to roommates?

No. Each person should be sent a separate invitation.

What if the roommates are siblings?

They may receive one invitation with their names listed alphabetically on separate lines.

Is it okay to have "No Children" printed on the invitation?

No, it is not. Instead, do not include children's names on the inner envelope. This is the proper way to distinguish this; however, many parents do not realize this fact. Have your friends and family spread the word that you do not wish to have children at the wedding.

May I include gift registry cards with the invitations?

No. It is acceptable to include these cards in your bridal shower invitations, so many guests will already know where you are registered. Have your families spread the word regarding your choices for gift registries to other guests.

We would really prefer money in lieu of gifts. Can we put this in the invitation?

Absolutely not. If you would prefer money, have your families be the ones to spread the word, but only if they are asked what you would prefer for a gift.

May I address my aunt and uncle as such on the inner envelope?
It is both proper and formal to use the titles Mr. and Mrs. (or appropriate titles) for all guests on the inner and outer envelopes. If your wedding is more casual, using aunt or uncle, or even the first names may be fine for the inner envelope.

Photography

I don't see how we can fit all those pictures in between the ceremony and reception. What is another option?
Taking photos (even of the bride and groom) before the ceremony is increasing in popularity. If you choose to do this, have your photographer take you someplace quiet and private when it is time for you and the groom to meet for the first time. This can still be a special moment for the two of you.

Reception

We have an uneven number of people in our wedding party. How do we do the wedding party dance?
The wedding party dance is not obligatory. If you choose to do this dance, have the bridal party dance with their spouses or dates.

I am having a small ceremony. Is it OK to invite more people to the reception?
Many couples are choosing to exchange vows in front of close friends and family only, or even alone. Yes, it is OK to issue invitations to the reception only if you would like to invite more people to the "party."

Do I have to invite work associates to my wedding?
You do not have to invite work associates. You can invite those whom you see socially. It is usually a good idea to invite your immediate supervisor.

Unexpected Situations

My stepfather has fallen ill, and probably won't be able to attend the wedding. What should I do?

You may choose to put the plans on hold until he is well, or you can continue on as planned (if this is suitable) and make special arrangements to deal with the matter. You may consider having another close relative stand in for him if he is part of the ceremony. You may wish to make mention of the situation or offer a prayer during the service. In addition, you can hold a viewing party of the video with him after the honeymoon.

My grandmother has fallen ill, and will probably pass away before our wedding date. She is quite dear to me and I can't imagine her not being there when I get married. What should I do?

You will need to determine if continuing with the plans is appropriate for your situation. Some brides and grooms have chosen to hold a civil or nondenominational ceremony at the person's bedside prior to the planned wedding festivities. In this case, the person has the opportunity to see you be married and celebrate a special moment with you.

My grandfather passed away unexpectedly. Should I continue with my wedding plans?

You should consult with your clergy and families to determine the best course of action. Deciding whether to continue with the celebration is a personal decision. Many feel to hold a large party is disrespectful, while others believe that the deceased would want you to continue on with the plans.

If you do not proceed with the wedding festivities, have a printer rush cancellation notices, and mail them out as soon as possible. If you do proceed with the festivities, you may choose to add a tribute or special poem commemorating this person at the ceremony, or make a toast to him at the reception.

TO OUR READERS

We hope that *How to "I Do"* has been a helpful guide during your wedding planning journey. If you have any constructive feedback, or any personal wedding planning experiences you would like to share with us, you can contact us at:

How to "I Do"
P.O. Box 842
El Segundo, CA 90245

-or-

E-mail: HowToIDo@Yahoo.com

Web site: www.howtoidoweddings.com

We appreciate your comments and suggestions, and with your help, look forward to making any future editions of *How to "I Do"* even better!

Notes:

Notes: